The Little Investor

A Tale of Making Money Grow

by

Ciprian Ipate

ISBN: 979-88-9170-088-8

Publisher: Bookllo Publishing

Contents

Introduction

Welcome to an incredible journey where you'll not only learn about money but also how to make it work for you, no matter if you're buying a comic book or saving for that video game you've been eyeing. Imagine setting off on an adventure, with your trusty guide, Max the Money Mogul, showing you the ropes of earning, saving, and spending wisely. Think of this as your treasure map, leading you to the secrets of financial success, peppered with thrilling activities and challenges along the way. Every page you turn opens the door to mastering your finances, making smart decisions, and even growing your savings, all while having a blast. So, let's dive into this world together, discovering the power of money and how it can take you on the most exciting adventure yet.

How This Book Works

Let's take a moment to talk about how this book is going to be your map to discovering all the secrets of money management, in a way that's as fun as embarking on an adventure to uncharted territories. It's designed to teach you, step by step, the ins and outs of handling your finances, in language that feels like a friend talking to you, not a textbook lecturing you.

Imagine you're on a quest, like the heroes in your favorite stories. Instead of battling dragons or searching for lost treasure, you're learning to conquer the world of money. This book is split into chapters, each focusing on different aspects of financial wisdom. From earning your first dollars to saving for something special, all the way to investing and smart spending, we're covering it all.

You might be wondering, "How can money be an adventure?" Well, every adventure starts with understanding the map and the tools at your disposal. That's exactly what this book aims to be for you - a treasure map, and each chapter a tool to help you navigate the sometimes tricky, yet exciting world of money.

Our journey together will involve a mix of stories, activities, and even games, all designed to make learning about money feel like playtime, not classroom time. Each chapter builds on the last, so you'll start with the basics and move up to more complex ideas, just like leveling up in a game.

The activities and games aren't just for fun, though they are definitely that! They're crafted to help you put into practice what you're learning. This hands-on approach ensures that by the end of this book, you won't just know about money – you'll know how to be smart with it, too.

We also believe that learning is more fun with a guide. That's why you'll meet Max the Money Mogul. Think of Max as your guide through the land of finance. He's here to share stories, offer advice, and be by your side as you embark on this learning adventure. Max has seen it all in the world of money and has plenty of wisdom to share.

But why should you care about managing money? Because knowing how to handle money is like having a superpower. It helps you make dreams come true, whether that's buying that video game you've been eyeing, saving up for college, or even starting your own business someday. Money isn't just paper and coins; it's freedom, opportunity, and the ability to make choices.

As we journey through each chapter, remember, there are no wrong questions. Curiosity is your compass here. If there's something you don't understand, that's an opportunity to explore deeper. Use the glossary at the back of the book if you stumble upon unfamiliar terms, and know that with each question, you're picking up another key to unlock the mysteries of money management.

While the journey through the world of money might seem long at first, remember every venture starts with a single step. And with each step, you'll gain more confidence. By the end of this book, you'll not only understand money better, you'll be equipped to make smart decisions with it – decisions that can shape your future in exciting ways.

So, as we set off on this adventure, keep an open mind, be ready to learn, and most of all, have fun. This isn't just about numbers and dollars; it's about setting the foundation for your dreams and learning how to achieve them.

This book is more than just words on pages. It's your interactive guide to becoming a young money mogul. By the time we close the final chapter, you'll have traveled far from where you started, equipped with the knowledge and skills to navigate the financial world confidently.

Remember, the path to becoming savvy about money is a journey, not a sprint. And it's a journey best enjoyed when taken at your own pace. So, feel free to linger on chapters that intrigue you, revisit concepts that challenge you, and most importantly, apply what you learn in real life.

So, are you ready to take the first step into the world of financial wisdom with Max and me? Let's turn the page and begin this extraordinary adventure together. Welcome to your journey into mastering money!

Meet Your Money Guide: Max the Money Mogul

Once upon a time, in a land not so far away, there lived a wise and adventurous soul named Max. Max wasn't your ordinary adventurer; he was a Money Mogul, known across lands far and wide for his knack for turning pennies into gold. He had a secret, though. His true wealth lay not in the coins that filled his treasure chest but in the knowledge and wisdom he had about money. And guess what? He's here to share that treasure with you.

Max has traveled through towering mountains of debt and sailed across vast oceans of savings. He's battled the fearsome dragons of expenses and unearthed hidden gems of investments. With a heart as golden as his coins, Max believes in the magic of sharing his wealth of knowledge with young adventurers like you.

"The journey of a thousand miles begins with a single penny," Max often says, winking. He knows that understanding money isn't just about counting digits or hoarding heaps of cash. It's about making smart choices, dreaming big, and taking small steps towards those dreams every day.

Max's tales are not just stories; they are lessons laced with adventure and wisdom. He'll take you on a journey through enchanted forests where savings grow on trees and guide you through mysterious caves where the secrets of smart spending are hidden.

His words are simple, yet they carry the power to transform. "It's not about how much you have but what you do with what you have," he often murmurs as he guides you across the perilous Bridge of Budgeting or the Cliffs of Credit.

But who is Max, you might wonder? Is he a wizard with a magic wand that turns everything into gold? Well, not exactly. Max used to be just like you. He made mistakes; he spent his entire allowance on things he didn't need, and he once thought saving was something only adults did. Through his adventures, though, he learned the true value of money. Now, he's here to pass those lessons onto you.

Why does Max care so much, you ask? Because he believes that every young adventurer has the potential to become a Money Mogul in their own right. He's seen too many people lost in the Forest of Financial Frustration, and if he can light a path for you to follow, he believes he's found his life’s true treasure.

Max will be your guide, your mentor, but most importantly, your friend. He'll share with you the Secrets of Saving, the Powers of Planning, and the Mysteries of Making Money Grow. He knows the challenges that lie ahead, but he also knows that within you lies the courage and the wisdom to overcome them.

Alongside Max, you'll embark on quests that will require you to think, to act, and to reflect. You'll learn the importance of setting goals, the thrill of achieving them, and the joy of using your resources to make the world a better place.

Max doesn’t promise the journey will always be easy. There will be monsters of debt that’ll try to trap you in their grasp and sirens of impulsive spending whose calls you’ll have to resist. But with Max by your side, armed with knowledge and a heart full of courage, you’ll navigate through these challenges.

He's ready to share his map with you, a map that will guide you through the realms of financial wisdom, from the Basics of Bucks to the Towers of Investments, from the Dungeons of Debt to the Castles of Credit Scoring.

Max believes that with the right knowledge, anyone, no matter how young, can master the art of money management. "The greatest wealth," he says, "is to live content with little, to seek elegance rather than luxury, and refinement rather than fashion. To be worthy, not respectable, and wealthy, not rich."

So, are you ready to join Max on this journey? To learn, to grow, and to embark on an adventure that’s not just about accumulating wealth but about discovering your true potential? Max believes in you, and he’s here to show you that the world of money, with all its mysteries and majesties, is within your grasp.

Remember, every coin you save, every wise choice you make, and every goal you reach brings you closer to becoming a Money Mogul in your own adventure. With Max as your guide, the path ahead is bright. The chapters that follow are your stepping stones. Let the adventure begin.

And so, with a twinkle in his eye and a coin magically flipping through his fingers, Max extends a hand, inviting you into a world where money isn't just pieces of paper or metal, but a tool, an ally, and a stepping stone to your dreams. "Let's make your journey extraordinary," he whispers. "Are you ready?"

The Basics of Bucks

Imagine you're on a quest, much like the heroes in your favorite stories, but this adventure is all about unlocking the mysteries of money. In this chapter, named "The Basics of Bucks," we're going to start our journey into the world of finance right at the beginning. Think of money as a tool, pretty much like a magic wand, that can help you achieve your dreams, big or small. But first, you need to know what it is. Money comes in many forms - the cash you might get for your birthday, the cards your parents swipe at the store, or even the digital dollars they use to buy things online. Next, we'll explore how everyone, from your neighbors to your parents, earns these dollars. It's like gathering your gear before venturing out. And to make it even more exciting, we'll set up a lemonade stand, not just any stand, but one with a budget, to learn how earning money works. So, let's gear up, adventurers, it's time to discover the treasure of knowledge buried in the "Basics of Bucks" and unwrap the secrets of earning, spending, and saving!

What is Money?

Imagine you're on a grand quest, much like the explorers and adventurers from the tales we love. On this quest, there's a tool so powerful, it can trade for almost anything in the world - this tool, my friends, is called money. In its essence, money is a promise, an agreement between people that it can be exchanged for things like toys, books, or even a slice of pizza. It's fascinating to think about, isn't it? Once upon a time, people traded what they had, like grains for wool, but as adventures grew and the world became a vast, interconnected kingdom, carrying chickens or heavy sacks of grain to trade became quite impractical. So, voilà! Money was created as a much easier way to trade. From shiny coins to paper bills, and now even digital numbers on a screen, money has transformed. It's like a shape-shifter from our favorite stories, changing forms but always holding onto its power to make trades easier and help people get what they need or desire. So, as we embark on this journey together, let's discover just how magical and useful this tool can be in the vast realm of our everyday lives and dreams.

Types of Money: Cash, Cards, and Digital Dollars Once upon a time, in the land of finance, there lived three very distinct types of money, each with its own tale and adventure. These were Cash, Cards, and the digital frontier, Digital Dollars. Our journey will take us through the mystical realms of each, exploring their strengths, weaknesses, and how they fit into the grand tapestry of commerce and trade.

In the beginning, there was **Cash**. Imagine holding a shiny coin or a crisp paper bill in your hand. It's tangible, real. You can touch it, smell it, and even hear the jingle of coins dancing in your pocket. Cash has been the foundation of trade, from ancient marketplaces to your local ice cream truck. It's immediate and universally accepted for a slice of pizza or a new comic book.

But as our kingdom of commerce grew, carrying all that treasure became cumbersome for knights and explorers alike. Then came the era of the **Cards**. These magical slabs of plastic were like carrying a chest of gold, but without the heavy lifting. With just a swipe or a tap, you could buy anything from a dragon's egg to sparkly crystals. Cards made money flexible, like a bendy sword, and allowed people to purchase things without the clink and clatter of real coins.

Yet, the greatest adventure lay beyond, in the realm of **Digital Dollars**. Imagine buying a starship or a unicorn, not by handing over coins or a card, but by sending magic spells through the air! Digital Dollars are the invisible money that lives in devices like smartphones and computers. With a click or a tap, you can send money flying over mountains and across oceans to land precisely where you wish it to go.

Each type of money has its guardians and challenges. **Cash**, though loved for its simplicity, must be guarded closely, as dragons and pickpockets alike have a keen interest in shiny, tangible wealth. Losing it is like losing a piece of your treasure chest.

The guardians of the **Cards** realm are the banks, noble institutions that promise to protect your wealth with spells of security. But beware! There are sorcerers who cast phishing spells and skimmers in the shadows, lurking to steal your card's magic.

In the digital kingdom, the guardians are more mystical, using codes and firewalls to protect the Digital Dollars. This realm is vast and full of wonders, but also dark webs where tricksters try to lure unsuspecting adventurers into giving away their precious digital treasure.

Yet, fear not! For with knowledge and wisdom, you can navigate these realms safely. Knowing when to use Cash for small treasures, Cards for larger bounties, and Digital Dollars for quests across the digital sea is all part of becoming a financial warrior.

As you embark on your own adventures, remember that each type of money has its time and place. **Cash** is perfect for a treasure you can hold, like a potion from the local apothecary. **Cards** can help you amass items from faraway lands without carrying a heavy purse. And **Digital Dollars** allow you to trade with merchants from the other side of the world, without ever leaving your castle.

But with great power comes great responsibility. Protecting your treasure from the dragons and thieves of the world will require courage, intelligence, and a bit of magic—learning the secrets of PINs, passwords, and the spells of cybersecurity.

As you grow in your journey, you'll learn to choose wisely between Cash, Cards, and Digital Dollars, mastering the art of transaction and trade. Each has its own path, its own story, but all are bound by the same quest – to serve in your grand adventures in the marketplace of life.

Remember, young squire, the type of money you choose on your quests shapes your journey. Will you carry a pouch of gold coins, a card imbued with the power of a thousand treasures, or command the invisible forces of Digital Dollars?

Your quest is just beginning, and the choices you make will lead to tales of heroism and adventure in the vast, evolving world of money. So wield your knowledge bravely, for it is the most powerful weapon in all your financial endeavors.

In the kingdom of finance, you are the hero of your own story. Whether trading with merchants in the bustling market squares or questing through the mystical world of online shopping, your journey will be filled with learning and excitement. Cash, Cards, and Digital Dollars are your tools and allies, each playing its part in your epic saga of commerce and discovery.

So venture forth, brave adventurer, with your head held high and your wallet wisely equipped. The realms of money await, full of trials to overcome and treasures to be found. And remember, in this grand adventure, the wealth you gain isn't just in your pocket – it's the knowledge and experience you gather along the way.

How People Earn Money

Imagine embarking on a treasure hunt, where every task you complete rewards you with pieces of gold. That's pretty much how people earn money in the real world, but instead of digging in hidden locations, they're using their skills and time. Some people solve puzzles with computers, others create magical stories or dishes that remind you of grandma's cooking, and there are those who help build bridges or design clothes. Every job is like a unique adventure, requiring a special set of tools - be it knowledge, creativity, or strength. The more you learn and practice, the better you become at tackling these quests. And just like any great adventure, the journey to earning money is filled with challenges to overcome and lessons to be learned, making the treasure at the end not just coins in your pocket, but the satisfaction of knowing you've grown stronger and smarter. So, as we step into the world of earning, let's keep our eyes wide open for the opportunities to learn, grow, and contribute, turning our adventures today into the treasures of tomorrow.

Activity: Lemonade Stand Budget Imagine it's a sunny Saturday morning, and you've decided that today is the perfect day to set up a lemonade stand in your front yard. But, like any successful adventure, this one needs a bit of planning first. Let's dive into how you can create a budget for your lemonade stand, turning this sunny day into a lesson in finance and fun.

Every great endeavor begins with understanding what you need. For your lemonade stand, you'll need lemons, sugar, water, and cups. Now, the first step in budgeting is figuring out how much of each you'll need and how much it'll cost. That means a trip to the grocery store - either in person or online - to check the prices.

Once you have the prices, it's time to do some math. If one lemon makes about 2 cups of lemonade and you plan to sell 50 cups, how many lemons will you need? Don't forget the sugar and how it'll sweeten the deal, both for your lemonade and your customers. The trick here is to buy just enough so you won't have too much left over. Waste not, want not, as they say.

Now, let's talk about the cups. Disposable cups can be cost-effective, but they're not very kind to our planet. Maybe you can find a budget-friendly, eco-friendly option? It's a small choice that can have a big impact, showing your customers you care about more than just profits.

Let's not forget about the cost of a sign. You need to let people know what you're selling and for how much. A bit of cardboard and some markers can go a long way. Here, creativity doesn't cost a thing but can attract many customers.

Adding all your costs together gives you a total investment needed to start. But how much should you charge for each cup to not only recoup your costs but also make some profit? This is where you'll need to do some competitor research. What are others charging for lemonade? Yes, this includes the stand two blocks down.

Setting the right price is a balance. Too high, and you might scare away thirsty folks. Too low, and you'll be working hard for very little money. Finding that sweet spot is key.

Remember, the goal isn't just to make money; it's to learn and have fun. Maybe you decide to donate a portion of your earnings to a local animal shelter or use it to fund your next big idea. It's your hard-earned money, after all. You get to choose what to do with it.

Through this lemonade stand, you'll learn about costs, profits, and pricing, but also about responsibility and generosity. These are big concepts wrapped in a simple glass of lemonade.

But what if not everything goes as planned? What if it rains, or what if you buy too many lemons? Part of budgeting is planning for the unexpected. Setting aside a little bit of your money as savings can help you manage these surprises without turning them into problems.

After your lemonade stand day is done, take a moment to reflect. How much did you earn? Were there any surprises? What would you do differently next time? This reflection is a crucial step in learning and growing from the experience.

Now, think about next steps. Maybe you partner with a friend to create a bigger stand or add new items to your menu. The world of entrepreneurship is vast and varied, and you've just taken your first step.

This lemonade stand might seem like a small thing, but it's more than that. It's about making decisions, solving problems, and learning the value of money. It's about dreaming big, taking risks, and maybe even discovering a passion for business.

And remember, every big business tycoon started somewhere - perhaps with a lemonade stand just like yours. So take this experience, learn from it, and who knows where your next venture will take you!

In conclusion, this activity isn't just about selling lemonade; it's a stepping stone into the world of financial education. By managing your little business, you're learning skills that will benefit you throughout life. So, pour yourself a glass of lemonade, raise it high, and toast to your success, both today and in all your future endeavors.

The lessons you learn from this lemonade stand are just the beginning. As you continue on in this book, you'll discover more ways to earn, save, and spend wisely. Each chapter builds on the last, just like every step in your lemonade stand adventure built on the one before it. Together, we're on a journey to financial smarts, adventure, and maybe a bit of lemonade-scented success.

Chapter 2: The Art of Saving

After diving into the basics of bucks, let's embark on an exciting journey to discover "The Art of Saving." Imagine you're on an adventure, where every coin you save is a stepping stone to uncharted territories and magical lands. Saving isn't just about putting money away; it's about setting sail towards your dreams, one small treasure at a time. Think of your piggy bank as a trusty sidekick, guarding your loot, and every time you drop a coin into it, you're one step closer to buying something really special—maybe that toy you've been eyeing, or a gift for someone you care about.

Saving teaches us patience and helps us learn the value of waiting for something we really want rather than spending all our treasure on things we might forget about tomorrow. It's like planting a seed and watching it grow; your savings will bloom over time, becoming something much bigger and more wonderful than you imagined. And guess what? You don't have to do it alone. Whether you choose a piggy bank to start your journey or open a savings account with a little help from your guardians, your money is safe, slowly growing while you dream big. So, let's get ready to explore the world of saving—to discover how it can be super, why it's important for your adventures, and find the perfect place to keep your growing treasure safe. Remember, every great explorer started with a single step, or in our case, a single coin.

Why Saving is Super

Imagine embarking on an adventure through a jungle filled with hidden treasures. Now, picture your piggy bank or savings account as the trusty map guiding you to these treasures. Saving money is like being a superhero in your own financial comic strip. It's super because it allows you to be ready for any adventure, whether it's buying that special toy you've had your eye on or saving up for something big, like a family vacation or your college fund. Every penny saved is like a step closer to your dreams, giving you the power to make choices and prepare for the unexpected. It might feel slow at times, like watching a plant grow, but with patience and dedication, you'll see how your savings flourish into something wonderful. Plus, learning to save now sets you up for a lifetime of superhero moves, making smart decisions with your money and reaching goals you set for yourself. So, let's dive into this adventure with a spirit of wonder, ready to discover the superpower of saving and all the amazing things you can achieve with it.

Activity: Saving for a Special Toy

Imagine this: there's a special toy you've had your eyes on for weeks. It's shiny, new, and all your friends are talking about it. But there's a twist – it costs more money than you have right now. What do you do? This is where our adventure in saving begins. Let's embark on a journey, not just to get that toy but to learn the power of patience and determination along the way.

First, let's figure out how much this special toy costs. Write down the price. Next to it, write down how much money you have right now. Seeing the difference between these two numbers might seem like looking at a mountain from the valley, but remember, every climber starts with a single step.

Now, think about how you usually get money. Is it from an allowance, doing chores, or maybe birthday money? List all the ways you can earn some cash. This is your map to the summit – the more paths you find, the quicker you'll reach the top.

Let's set some milestones. If the toy is $50 and you have $10, you need to save $40. Break that down into smaller goals. Maybe you aim to save $10 each week. That means in just four weeks, you could have enough. Small goals make the journey seem less daunting and much more doable.

Where to keep your growing treasure? A piggy bank is a classic choice, but any secure container will do. Label it with a picture of your toy to keep your eyes on the prize. Every coin you add brings you closer to your goal.

Patience is key. It can be tempting to spend your money on small things here and there. Resist the urge. Remind yourself that every dollar spent on something else is a step away from your special toy.

Get creative in finding ways to add to your savings. Maybe offer to help out more around the house, or see if neighbors need any chores done. Each task is a mini-adventure, adding not just to your savings but to your experiences.

Keep track of your progress. Make a chart or a list and fill it in as you go. Seeing how far you've come can be a huge motivator to keep pushing forward. Celebrate those little victories – they're important.

Share your goal with family and perhaps even friends. Sometimes they might offer you extra chores for more money, or better yet, they'll become your cheerleaders on this journey, offering encouragement and support when you're feeling impatient.

Imagine finally having saved enough for your toy. The moment you've been waiting for has arrived. How do you feel? Proud, excited, maybe even a little surprised at how you made it happen? This feeling is your reward, even more so than the toy.

When the day comes to buy your toy, take a moment to reflect on the journey. You planned, worked hard, stayed disciplined, and finally achieved your goal. These are skills that will serve you well beyond this toy. They're the building blocks for any future dream.

Now, with the toy in your hands, consider the value of money and the effort it took to save it. You'll likely appreciate your toy even more, knowing the journey it took to get it.

This adventure in saving for a special toy is more than just a lesson in finances; it's a journey in character building. You've shown yourself to be patient, disciplined, creative, and determined. Remember these qualities, for they will help you climb many more mountains in the future.

Lastly, don't forget to dream big. Today it was a toy, but tomorrow it could be anything you set your mind to. Your potential is limitless, and your journey in financial wisdom has only just begun. Here's to many more adventures and dreams realized. Keep saving, keep learning, and keep reaching for those stars.

Remember, every big achievement starts with a simple step. You've taken the first step on a great adventure, not just to buy a toy but towards understanding money and its value. Carry these lessons forward, and who knows what you'll be saving for next? The possibilities are endless.

Places to Keep Your Money Safe

Imagine you've just found a shining, magical coin on a thrilling adventure, tucked away in the soft earth beneath a grand, ancient tree. Holding it tightly in your hand, you think, "Where should I keep this treasure safe?" Just like knights of old hid their gleaming gold away from prying eyes, you too have secret spots to shield your riches. One might be a piggy bank, sitting proudly on your shelf, guarding your coins with a stern but friendly smile. Another, more grown-up place, is a savings account at a bank, where your money doesn't just stay safe; it grows like a tiny seed into a towering tree. In a piggy bank, your money waits quietly for your next grand adventure. But in a savings account, it goes on its own journey, working hard and growing bit by bit, ready to surprise you with how much it has grown when you next need it. Both places keep your money safe, but they offer different paths for your treasure. Choosing where to keep your money is like choosing the path for your adventure. One path might lead you through a sunny glade; the other through a mysterious, twinkling cave. Each has its wonders to explore.

Piggy Banks vs. Savings Accounts Welcome back! We've been on a thrilling journey through the world of money, learning about how it works and the different ways we can be smart with it. Today, we're exploring two heroes in the realm of savings: piggy banks and savings accounts. While both are champions in their own right, they come with their own set of powers and adventures. Let's dive in!

Imagine your piggy bank as a brave knight, standing guard over your precious coins and bills. This knight is always there when you need it, right in your room. It's super easy to feed it some money, and whenever you want to check how much you've saved, you just flip it over and shake out its contents. There's something magical about seeing and touching your money, watching your savings grow right before your eyes. It's tangible, real, and incredibly encouraging.

But, as in any adventure story, there are limitations. Your piggy bank, strong as it may seem, can only protect your money up to a point. It doesn't have the power to multiply your savings or guard them against the sneaky thief, inflation, which slowly but surely reduces the value of your money over time. It's a valiant guard, but its skills are, let's say, a bit old-fashioned.

On the flip side of our tale, enter the mighty savings account, a powerful wizard in the world of finance. This wizard lives in a grand fortress called a bank or credit union. Unlike our knight, the savings account wizard can do something truly magical with your money - it can grow it. This magic comes in the form of interest, a small reward that the bank gives you for keeping your money with them. It's like your money is having its own little adventures and bringing back treasures from its journey.

Opening a savings account might seem like stepping into an enchanted forest. You'll likely need a grown-up to help you navigate this path since it involves setting up an account in your name. But once you're in, you're not alone. Your money is safe, insured by a powerful protection spell known as FDIC insurance in the United States, meaning even if the bank faces trouble, your money up to a certain amount is secure.

However, accessing your money isn't as simple as tipping over a piggy bank. You might need to visit the bank, use an ATM, or log in to an online account. This process can be a bit of an adventure itself, requiring patience and planning. It teaches you discipline and the art of waiting, valuable traits in any hero's journey.

Another enchanting aspect of the savings account is its ability to be part of bigger financial journeys. Like portals to new worlds, you can set up multiple accounts for different goals: one for saving for a new bike, another for that video game you've been eyeing, and even one for college. Each adventure, carefully planned and eagerly awaited.

But, no adventure is without its challenges. Savings accounts usually offer a modest interest rate, meaning your money grows slowly. It’s a patient wizard, not a flashy one. And, depending on the rules of the fortress (bank), there might be minimum balance requirements or fees that can nibble away at your savings like mischievous sprites.

So, how do you choose between the valiant knight and the powerful wizard? The truth is, you don't have to. In the quest of savings, having both a piggy bank and a savings account is like having a sword and a spellbook. They complement each other, each offering different lessons and joys. Your piggy bank can be for immediate goals, a visual and tactile reminder of the importance of saving. And your savings account? It's your long-term ally, growing your savings slowly but surely, preparing you for bigger adventures ahead.

Embarking on this dual adventure teaches you balance. You learn the excitement of saving for the near future with your piggy bank while also understanding the patience and foresight required for saving in a bank account. It's a combination of seeing your efforts pay off now and knowing they'll benefit you even more later on.

Remember, every hero’s journey starts with a single step. Whether it's putting your first coin into your piggy bank or depositing your first dollar in your savings account, you're beginning an epic adventure in the world of savings. Your actions today are laying down the path to your future dreams and goals.

As your savings grow, so will you. You'll learn about responsibility, the value of money, and the power of patience. Every deposit, no matter how small, is a victory, a step towards becoming a financial wizard in your own right. And who knows? Maybe one day, your journey in saving will inspire tales of its own.

Both piggy banks and savings accounts offer their own unique adventures in the world of saving money. By understanding the strengths and limitations of each, you can make smart choices that align with your goals and dreams. Remember, the choices you make today are the foundation of your financial future. So choose wisely, save diligently, and let your savings journey be one of the most epic tales ever told.

In the end, whether you choose the piggy bank, the savings account, or both, you're on the path to becoming a true hero in the story of your financial life. Each coin saved, each deposit made, is a step towards conquering your financial dragons and reaching your treasure-filled castles in the sky. So keep saving, keep dreaming, and let your financial adventure unfold in all its glory.

Chapter 3: Making Money Grow

Imagine you've planted a tiny seed in the ground, covered it with soil, and started watering it. Each day, you see it grow a bit more until one day, it's a huge tree bearing delicious fruits. That's exactly how making money grow works! It sounds like magic, doesn't it? But it's real. In this chapter, we'll explore the enchanting world of interest – it's like the water and sunshine for your money seed. You'll learn how leaving your money in certain places, like a savings account, can help it grow over time. We're not stopping at just saving; we're going to dive into the basics of investing too. Think of it like planting more seeds in different types of soil to see which one grows the best. You'll get to play a pretend stock market game that'll show you the ropes of investing without having to risk any real money. By the end of this adventure, you'll see that making your money grow isn't just a dream. It's something you can start doing today, and it's as thrilling as embarking on a quest to find buried treasure.

The Magic of Interest

Imagine you have a magical seed that could grow into a money tree, but instead of needing water and sun to grow, it grows more with time. That's the magic of interest! When you save your money in certain places, like a savings account, it's like planting a magical seed. Over time, the bank pays you a little extra money for keeping your savings with them. This extra money is called interest. It might start small, but just like a tree, it can grow bigger and stronger the longer you let it grow. So, every dollar you save is like a loyal friend that works to make more friends for you, without you having to do anything extra! It's your very own financial adventure where your money embarks on a journey to multiply, showing you the wonders of patience and the power of letting your money work for you. This magic trick of making money grow with interest can turn your dreams into reality, bit by bit, showing you that with time and patience, even the smallest savings can turn into a treasure chest.

Activity: Interest Exploration with Max's Savings

Let's embark on an adventure, one filled with the wonder of growing money. Imagine Max, our guide into the world of finances, has saved a hefty sum of money from his lemonade stand earnings. Instead of spending it all at once, Max is taking us on a journey to discover the magic of interest.

Now, what's this thing called interest? Think of it as a reward you get for letting someone else use your money. It's like if you lent a video game to a friend, and when they returned it, they gave you another game to play with for a while as a thank you. In the world of saving, banks are the friends, your saved money is the borrowed game, and the interest is the extra game you get to play with. Pretty neat, right?

Max decides to put his saved money into a savings account that offers interest. Over time, not only does he still have the money he saved, but he also has extra money – all because he was patient and smart with his savings. The excitement in Max's heart blooms like a flower in spring. This is the magic of saving and earning interest.

Let's break it down with a simple exploration. Imagine Max saved $100. The bank offers him 5% interest every year. That means, after one year, Max would have an extra $5, just because he kept his money in the bank. It's as if the money has grown on its own!

This might sound small, but here's where it gets fascinating. Let's say Max leaves his money and the interest he earned in the bank for another year. Now, he's earning interest not only on his original $100 but also on the $5 interest from the first year. This is called compound interest, and it's like magic. Over time, it makes money grow faster and bigger, like a snowball rolling down a hill.

To make this exploration more fun, Max decides to chart his money's growth on a graph. He draws a line that slowly, but steadily, goes up, representing his growing savings. This graph doesn't just show numbers increasing; it tells a story of patience, foresight, and the rewards of being wise with money.

Inspired by Max's journey, he and his friends decide to embark on a quest. They all pledge to save a portion of their allowances or earnings in a savings account. They meet every few months to share their stories of growth, not just in their savings but in their understanding of money.

Through Max's adventure, we learn something crucial: saving money isn't just about setting it aside. It's about making it grow, understanding the value of patience, and seeing firsthand the rewards of being financially savvy. And the best part? It's an adventure that we can all embark on, no matter how small our savings might be to start.

So, how can you start your adventure like Max? It's simple! Start by saving a little from what you earn or get as an allowance. Talk to your parents about opening a savings account that earns interest. And most importantly, be patient and let your money grow.

But remember, the journey of saving and growing money is unique to everyone. Maybe you're saving for a new bicycle, a video game, or even for college. No matter what your goals are, understanding and using the power of interest can help you reach them more efficiently.

Max's adventure in saving teaches us an invaluable lesson. With a dash of patience, a sprinkle of diligence, and the magic of interest, our own savings can grow beyond our imagination. It encourages us to dream big, start small, and keep going.

As we wrap up this exploration with Max, let's carry forward the spark of curiosity and the will to take smart financial steps. Who knows? One day, you might look back and thank your younger self for being brave, wise, and patient, just like Max.

And so, Max's journey continues, as does ours. With each day, we have the opportunity to make smart choices with our money, learn more, and watch our savings blossom. The adventure of understanding and leveraging interest is just the beginning. Let the wonder of growing your savings inspire you to explore further, dream bigger, and reach higher.

Remember, every great journey begins with a single step. Let Max's story inspire you to take your first step towards a future of financial wisdom and prosperity. Happy saving!

Simple Investments for Young Investors

Imagine your piggy bank could magically fill up faster just by being smart about where you put your money. That's kind of what investing is like! Just like how a tiny acorn grows into a gigantic oak tree, the money you invest can grow over time too. Think of investing as planting your money seeds in different places, like in companies or projects that can grow. It's like being part of a treasure hunt where, with patience and a bit of wisdom, the X marks the spot for a brighter future. You don't have to be a grown-up to start; all you need is a dash of curiosity, a sprinkle of dream, and a willingness to learn. Whether you're saving up for that ultra-cool bike or aiming for superhero status in the gaming world, starting to invest now can help turn your big dreams into reality. Remember, the adventure begins with a single step—or in this case, a single penny. So, let's set sail on this exciting journey of making your money grow, turning those pennies into treasure chests of possibilities!

Activity: Pretend Stock Market Game Welcome to a thrilling adventure where you're about to become a young investor on a journey through the wondrous world of the stock market. Imagine a place where companies grow like towering trees in a lush forest, and your goal is to pick the seeds (stocks) that will grow into the mightiest oaks.

First things first, let's understand what a stock is. Think of it as a tiny piece of a company. If the company does well, so does your piece of it. But if the company doesn't do too hot, neither does your stock. It's like choosing players for your basketball team, hoping they'll score tons of points.

Now, how do we start this game? We'll create our *pretend* stock market. You won't need real money, so no worries about dipping into your savings from that lemonade stand. Instead, you'll use play money to buy and sell stocks based on real companies that we'll track over time.

Let's gather some tools. You'll need some paper, a pen, and a ruler to create your investment journal. Plus, a bit of imagination will come in handy. Chart your own or use a template to keep track of your stocks. You'll play the role of an investor, deciding which stocks to buy or sell based on how you think the company will perform.

Here's the kicker: you're not alone in this adventure. You'll compete against your friends to see who can grow their pretend portfolio the most. Will you take risks on unknown companies, or stick with tried-and-true giants? The choice is yours, young investor.

To start, pick three companies you know. Maybe you choose a tech giant because you love their gadgets, or a fast-food chain because their fries are your go-to treat. Research them a little. What makes them tick? How have they been doing recently?

Next, you'll "buy" your stocks. Each player starts with the same amount of pretend money. Decide how much of it you want to spend on each company's stock. Remember, don't put all your eggs in one basket; spreading out your investments can help you not lose all your money if one stock goes down.

Keep an eye on your companies. Every week, check how their real stocks are doing online (with a parent's help) or in the newspaper's business section. Are they going up or down? This will tell you how your pretend stocks are performing.

Time to buy or sell! As you watch your stocks, you may decide to sell some and buy others. Maybe you hear news that one of your companies is about to launch something big. Do you invest more, thinking their stock will shoot up? It's all part of the strategy.

At the end of the game, after a set time you decide on, see who made the most pretend money. There will be ups and downs, but that's part of the excitement. The stock market can be unpredictable, but it's also full of opportunities.

This game isn't just about winning or losing fake money; it's about understanding the ups and downs of investing. It's a journey that requires patience, research, and a bit of courage. Every decision you made was a step towards learning how investments work in the real world.

Reflect on your journey. What worked for you? What didn't? Maybe you found that diversifying your portfolio really helped, or perhaps being bold paid off. Write these reflections in your investment journal. They're valuable lessons for the future.

Finally, share your stories. What were the biggest surprises? Did any company perform in a way you didn't expect? Discussing with your friends can help you all learn from each other and become wiser investors for the next round of the game.

In wrapping up our pretend stock market game, remember, the real prize isn't the pretend money you ended up with. It's the knowledge and skills you've gained. You've taken the first steps on an exciting path. The world of investing is full of adventures, challenges, and opportunities. Keep exploring, keep learning, and who knows? Maybe one day, you'll be ready to invest for real. For now, you've earned a big round of applause for taking on the challenge and expanding your financial horizons.

Remember, young investor, the journey you've embarked on is one of discovery and growth. You've begun to unlock the mysteries of the stock market, and that's something to be incredibly proud of. Keep dreaming big, stay curious, and continue to seek adventures in all that you do. The world of finance is vast and waiting for you to explore it further. Until then, keep your investment journal close, your mind open, and your spirit ready for the next big adventure.

Chapter 4: Wise Spending

Imagine you've just found a treasure chest, but instead of gold and jewels, it's filled with all the things you've ever wished for. Sounds dreamy, right? Now, what if I told you that learning the art of wise spending could be your key to unlocking that chest? You see, every time you get money, whether from your allowance, a birthday, or a lemonade stand, you're standing at a crossroads. One path is splurging on every whim—like a giant candy bar that disappears in a flash. The other is weighing your wants against your needs, akin to choosing a sturdy backpack that'll carry your adventures for years. Wise spending doesn't mean you can't have fun; it means making choices that bring you the most joy and value in the long run. Imagine being a superhero where your power is making smart shopping decisions, like comparing prices or waiting for a sale on that video game you've been eyeing. This chapter is like your training ground, where you'll learn to distinguish between needs and wishes, and how to be a champion of smart shopping. So, let's embark on this adventure together, and who knows? You might just find that spending wisely is more magical than any treasure chest.

Needs vs. Wishes

Imagine you're setting sail on a grand adventure, with your pockets full of gold coins. Now, these coins aren't just regular coins; they're your ticket to everything you'll encounter on your journey. But here's the kicker: your backpack can only carry so much, and you've got to decide whether to pack the essentials - your needs, like a sturdy compass, fresh water, and a map, or fill it with wishes - maybe a fancy telescope with golden trim or a chest of shimmering jewels. It's fun to think about having all those exquisite things, isn't it? But when the path gets twisty and you're trying to navigate through the wild, it's the essentials, the needs, that will guide you home. Just like on our imaginary expedition, every day we face decisions about how to spend our real treasure, our money. Learning to tell apart what we truly need to make it through the day, and what we just wish we could have, is like learning how to pack our backpack for the greatest adventure of all. By choosing wisely, you save room (and coins!) for what truly matters, ensuring your journey is both thrilling and rewarding.

Activity: Budget for a Birthday Party Imagine you've been planning the most amazing birthday party in your head for weeks. The vision's there, complete with your favorite games, decorations, and, of course, the most delicious cake. But, how do you make this dream party a reality? With a budget, that's how! Let's dive into how you can plan a fantastic birthday party without breaking your piggy bank.

First, take a deep breath and think about what makes a party truly special to you. Is it having all your friends around, playing fun games, or maybe it's the magic of blowing out the candles on a cake that's just too yummy to not dream about at night? Keep in mind; a memorable party doesn't mean you have to spend a lot of money.

Now, with those special elements in mind, grab a piece of paper and let's start listing them down. But here's the kicker – next to each item, write down an estimated cost. You might wonder, "How do I know how much everything costs?" Here's where a bit of detective work comes in! You can ask adults, look up prices online (with supervision), or even call places like bakeries to get an idea.

Don't worry if the numbers start adding up quickly; it happens to the best of party planners. Here's where we start thinking creatively. Maybe instead of a store-bought cake, you could bake one with family or friends. Not only could this save money, but it's also an adventure in the making and a priceless memory in the baking!

With our list and estimated costs in front of us, it's time to set a total budget. This is the maximum amount of money you're able to spend on your party. It might come from savings, gifts, or maybe a bit of both. The important part is sticking to this number once it's set.

Now comes a bit of magic – prioritizing. Look at your list and start to rank each item based on what's most important to you. Essential items like cake and decorations might stay, but maybe you realize, instead of a magician, you can create your own magic show.

As you tweak your list, you'll see your budget start to take a shape that looks doable. This might mean making some tough choices, like maybe having a smaller guest list or choosing games that don't cost a penny but are just as fun.

If the numbers still aren't adding up, it's time to get really imaginative. What if, instead of buying decorations, you and your friends make them? Or maybe there's a talent among your family members for face painting—suddenly, you've got entertainment that's both personal and free!

A big part of being smart with your party budget is understanding the value of things. Sure, a professional DJ sounds cool, but a playlist of your favorite songs that everyone can dance to brings the party to life just as much – and costs nothing but a bit of time to create.

With your adjusted list and budget in hand, it's time to start putting the plan into action. If you've decided on baking a cake, gather those recipes. If you're crafting decorations, what supplies will you need? This is where your budget helps keep you on track and makes sure you're not overspending.

Remember, part of being a great budgeter is being flexible. Sometimes, things might not go exactly as planned, and that's okay. Maybe you find out paper for decorations is on sale, and you can get more bang for your buck. Or perhaps a friend offers to bring a game they have, reducing your expenses even further.

The day of the party is here, and as you look around at the decorations you made, the cake that's waiting to be devoured, and your friends laughing and playing games, you'll feel a sense of pride. Not just because you threw an awesome party, but because you did it while being smart about your spending.

This experience isn't just about having fun; it's a lesson in creativity, planning, and financial responsibility. These are skills that will come in handy not just for parties, but for many aspects of life.

So, as you blow out the candles on your cake, make a wish, but also take a moment to appreciate the journey you took to get here. You've learned that with a bit of creativity and smart planning, you can make magic happen, no matter what your budget is.

In the end, the most important thing about a birthday party – or any celebration – isn't how much you spend, but the joy and memories it brings. You've shown that, with thoughtful planning and a dash of imagination, you can create moments that you and your friends will remember for years to come. And that, my friend, is priceless.

So, what are you waiting for? Your next adventure in budgeting and planning is just around the corner. Whether it's for your next birthday party or another exciting project, you've got the tools and know-how to make it amazing. Go out there and show the world how creative and savvy you can be!

Smart Shopping Tips

Imagine you're on a quest, a quest for the perfect gift or that must-have gadget. You've saved up your coins, and now it's time to make them work as hard as they can. Think of shopping like a puzzle; looking for the best deals is part of solving it. Before you set off, make a list of what you need – this keeps your eyes on the prize and helps you avoid getting distracted by other shiny things. Comparing prices between stores is like a treasure hunt; sometimes, the same item can cost less at a different shop or online! And remember, ads are like sirens trying to lure you in with their songs – they make things look more appealing than they might actually be. Coupons and sales are your allies in this adventure, helping you stretch your coins even further. But, the ultimate magic trick? Asking yourself if you really need it or if it's just a wish that might fade. This way, you turn into a smart shopper, not just spending wisely, but spending magically, making every coin count in your epic journey.

Activity: Price Comparison Challenge As we continue our adventure through wise spending, it's time to embark on an exciting quest. It's not just any quest, but a special challenge that will sharpen your shopping skills and turn you into a savvy spender. Imagine you're on a treasure hunt, but instead of gold and jewels, you're searching for the best deals and prices.

Let's set the scene. Imagine you've been saving for that one awesome toy. You've been dreaming about it, visualizing the moment you finally get to play with it. But here's the twist – you want to maximize your savings and get the best deal out there. That's where the Price Comparison Challenge comes into play.

The mission, should you choose to accept it, involves becoming a detective in your own right. You'll need to investigate, compare, and uncover the best prices for the toy you've been longing for. But how, you might wonder? Don't worry, I've got you covered with the steps to success.

First, grab a notebook or a piece of paper. This will be your detective's logbook. Write down the name of the toy or item you're saving for at the top of the page. Excitement bubbles inside you as you prepare to embark on this adventure. Remember, this isn't just about buying a toy; it's about becoming wise in the ways of spending and saving.

Next, it's time to hunt for prices. Use the internet with the help of an adult, or check out store flyers to find different places that sell your desired toy. Write down all the prices you find in your logbook. Look out for sales or promotions – they can be your allies in this challenge.

Now, consider the condition. Sometimes, items are sold used or refurbished at a lower price. Decide if you're only looking for new items or if you're okay with pre-owned ones. This decision can make a big difference in what you find.

It's not just about the sticker price, though. Consider other factors like shipping costs or tax if you're ordering online. Sometimes, a lower price at first glance isn't the best deal after adding these extra costs. Record all this information in your logbook like a true detective.

After gathering all your evidence, it's time to compare. Lay out all the information you've collected. Seeing it all in one place will help you uncover the best deal. You're almost there, the thrill of the hunt tingling in your veins.

But wait! Before you make your final decision, there's one more step. Think about saving a bit longer for a high-quality version of your toy. Sometimes, paying a little more upfront can save you money in the long run because the item lasts longer or works better.

Once you've decided where the best deal is, discuss your findings with a parent or guardian. They can offer advice, help you think through your decision, and even assist in the final purchase. Your teamwork can turn this individual quest into a collaborative adventure.

With your investigation complete and your decision made, it's time to make the purchase. But the journey doesn't end here. After buying your toy, reflect on the process. What did you learn? How did it feel to hunt for the best price and save money?

This Price Comparison Challenge isn't just a one-time adventure. It's a skill you can use for the rest of your life. Whether you're saving for a bicycle, a video game, or even much later in life when you're buying a car or house, being a smart shopper can save you tons of money.

So there you have it, young adventurer. You've not only worked towards buying something you really wanted, but you've also learned an invaluable skill. This challenge has equipped you with the knowledge to make smart spending decisions, setting you up for a future of wise financial choices.

In this journey, you've experienced firsthand that spending wisely isn't about denial; it's about making thoughtful decisions. It's about understanding the value of money and making it work for you in the best way possible. And remember, every smart decision you make, no matter how small, builds the path to a secure and prosperous future.

Now, with your newfound skill and confidence, what will be your next Price Comparison Challenge? The world of smart spending awaits you, filled with opportunities to save, learn, and grow. Embrace it with enthusiasm, for you're now not just a spender but a wise spender. The adventures and lessons learned on this journey will serve you well, far beyond the realm of money and into the broader journey of life.

The Give, Save, Spend Plan

Imagine you've just found a glittering treasure chest, filled not only with gold but with the secrets to managing it wisely. That's what we're diving into in this chapter. The Give, Save, Spend Plan is like having a map to navigate through the world of money - it helps you make smart choices about what to do with your cash. First up, we'll learn how to balance your treasure. Think of your money as being split into three jars: one for giving, one for saving, and the last one for spending. It's like playing a game where every coin you get has to be placed in one of these jars, and each has its own special purpose. Next, we'll explore the joy of giving. It might seem like putting coins into the 'give' jar takes away from your treasure, but you'll find out how sharing can actually make your heart and someone else's, a whole lot richer. And lastly, we'll tackle why saving some of that treasure for later is just as thrilling as spending it right now. You'll set off on an adventure, creating your very own Give, Save, Spend jars, understanding that money isn't just about buying stuff—it's about creating happiness for yourself and others. So, let's set sail towards mastering this magical plan, where every decision you make with your money can lead to new discoveries and joyous journeys.

Balancing Your Money

Imagine your money as a cake. If you eat all of it at once, you won't have any left for later. Similarly, spending all your money as soon as you get it leaves nothing for your future self. In the 'Give, Save, Spend Plan,' you learn to slice your cake—er, money—into three perfect parts. Think of it like this: one slice goes into a jar for spending on things you need or want now. The second slice is tucked away in a savings jar, growing bigger over time for things in the future. And the third? It's for giving, sharing a piece of your cake with someone who needs it more. Balancing your money is like being the master of a game, a game where the goal is to make sure every part of your life is taken care of—your present self, your future dreams, and the world around you. So, start thinking like a money-balancing hero. Every dime you get is a chance to make magic happen, dividing it up not just because you have to, but because it's the secret to making your money cake last and taste sweeter with every bite.

Activity: Create Your Own Give, Save, Spend Jars Embarking on an adventure, we find ourselves in a world where every coin and dollar bill holds the promise of possibility. This journey isn't just about hoarding treasure; it's about learning to manage it wisely, ensuring that each piece of gold (or, in our case, money) finds its rightful place, whether it be in the realms of giving, saving, or spending.

Imagine, if you will, three enchanted jars, each with its own purpose and power. The first one glimmers with the light of generosity - the Give jar. The second, fortified with the strength of foresight, is the Save jar. And the third, sparkling with the excitement of immediate delight, is the Spend jar. Our quest today is to bring these jars from the realm of imagination into our world.

To start this venture, you will need three jars. These can be any kind of containers you have around the house - old jam jars, mason jars, or even coffee containers. The most important thing is that they are clear, so you can see your treasure accumulate over time. Next, you'll need to gather some supplies to decorate your jars. Think about stickers, markers, glitter, or whatever craft supplies you fancy. This is your adventure, after all, and these jars should reflect your personality and spirit.

Once you have your jars and decorations ready, it's time to label each one. Take a marker and write 'Give' on the first jar. This jar is for money you wish to donate to help others - perhaps to support a local animal shelter, to contribute to a community project, or to offer a gift to someone in need. The 'Save' jar is next; this is where you'll stash money for future dreams and desires, like that special toy you've been eyeing, or to have some savings for a rainy day. Finally, label the last jar 'Spend.' This is for money you can use anytime for small purchases, like a new book or a treat from the ice cream truck.

Now comes the fun part: personalizing your jars. With your craft supplies at the ready, start decorating each jar according to its purpose. Maybe the Give jar gets adorned with stickers that represent love and care, while the Save jar could have images of things you're saving up for, and the Spend jar might be decorated with items you enjoy buying. Let your creativity flow as you make each jar uniquely yours.

With your jars decorated and labeled, it's time to set them up in a special place in your home where you'll see them every day. This could be on a shelf in your room, on a desk, or anywhere else that's easily accessible. The important thing is that they remind you of your goals and inspire you every day to make smart money decisions.

The final step in this adventure is to start using your jars. Each time you receive money, be it from a birthday card, doing chores, or from your lemonade stand profits, think about how you want to divide it among the jars. There's no right or wrong way to do this; it's all about what feels right to you and your goals. Maybe you decide to split your money evenly among the jars, or perhaps some weeks you'll feel inspired to give a little more to one jar over the others.

As you continue to fill your jars, you'll see your progress right before your eyes. The magic of watching your savings grow, your spendable cash accumulate, and your charitable fund increase will inspire you to keep going, to keep dividing your money in ways that support your dreams, your wants, and your ability to make a difference.

Remember, these jars are more than just containers; they're a symbol of your journey toward becoming wise with your money. Each time you make a decision on how to allocate your funds, you're learning invaluable lessons about budgeting, saving, and giving back.

This activity is just the beginning. As you grow older, the lessons you learn from your Give, Save, Spend jars will evolve with you. Someday, your jars might turn into bank accounts, and your contributions might grow larger, but the principles will remain the same. You'll always have the power to make thoughtful decisions with your money, impacting not just your own future, but also the world around you.

So take pride in your Give, Save, Spend jars, for they are a testament to your journey into financial wisdom. They represent not just where you're going, but also who you'll become: a person of compassion, foresight, and smart spending habits. Let these jars be a beacon, guiding you through the adventures of life with the confidence of someone who knows the value of a dollar, not just in the wealth it brings, but in the good it can do.

In the end, these jars are more than an activity; they're a stepping stone on your path to mastering the art of money management. They teach us that with a bit of creativity, discipline, and heart, managing money can be an exciting adventure – one that leads to a future bright with possibilities. So let's treasure these lessons, and may the journey of financial enlightenment continue to be a thrilling adventure, filled with growth, learning, and the joy of giving, saving, and spending wisely.

The Joy of Giving

Imagine standing on the edge of a magical forest, where every tree is a towering giant made of gleaming gold and silver, and every leaf could buy a mountain of your favorite candy. This forest, though, holds a secret more precious than gold itself: the joy of giving. As you journey through the dense, whispering leaves, you might find yourself wondering why sharing your treasures could ever be as thrilling as discovering them. Yet, the magical creatures of this forest know that giving isn't just about parting with something you own; it's about embarking on an adventure that lights up another's world in ways you might never have imagined.

Think of the time you helped a friend in need, shared a favorite toy, or simply lent an ear to someone who felt alone. Didn't it feel like your heart grew a little warmer, a little brighter? That's because giving taps into an enchanted power we all hold within—the power to spread joy, forge stronger bonds, and weave a tapestry of kindness that covers the globe. It's not always about giving away your possessions but sharing something far more valuable: your time, your attention, and your care.

So, as we nestle this idea next to the plans to save and spend wisely, remember that your arsenal of treasures is never diminished by sharing. In fact, it grows in ways that are invisible to the eye but can be felt with every beat of your heart. Together, let's embark on this heartwarming quest, discovering the boundless riches that await when you open your heart to the joy of giving. Who knows what adventures lie ahead when we set sail on this journey? The paths are many, the skies are wide, and every step taken in kindness is a step towards a brighter, more magical world.

Activity: Planning a Giving Project Imagine you're on an adventure, not in a deep, dark jungle or on a high mountain, but a journey that might just change someone's life, including yours. In this chapter, we're going to embark on a special mission called the Giving Project. It's not just any task; it's your chance to sprinkle a little bit of happiness and light into the world using something all of us can share—our generosity.

First things first, let's dream up our project. Think of it like painting a picture. What would you love to see in the world? Maybe everyone at your school has enough to eat for lunch, or the animals at the local shelter feel loved and cared for. This is your canvas, so you decide the beautiful scene you want to create.

Now, with our picture in mind, we need to sketch out our plans. Every great adventure needs a map, and this is no different. Ask yourself, who will your project help? How will it make a difference? And very importantly, what will you need to bring your vision to life? This might include time, volunteers, or even a bit of money.

Let's talk about the treasure chest for this journey—funding. There are many ways to gather the resources you need. Maybe you can save a portion of your allowance, do extra chores for family and neighbors, or even organize a small fundraiser like a bake sale or a car wash. Remember, every little bit helps and adds up to make a big difference.

But a captain never sails alone. Gather a crew of friends, family, or classmates who are just as excited about your project as you are. Together, brainstorm how you can make the most impact. More heads are better than one, and this can make your adventure even more fun and meaningful.

Now, envision setting sail. It's time to put your plans into action. This might mean packing lunches for those who need it, spending time at the animal shelter, or whatever your project entails. While you work, pay attention to how it makes you feel. Are you excited? Happy to be helping others? These feelings are the true treasure of our journey.

Every explorer keeps a logbook, and you should too. Track your progress, jot down what works well, and think about what you might do differently next time. This will be invaluable for your next giving project, and yes, there should definitely be a next time!

After your project comes to an end, take a moment to reflect. Gather your crew and talk about the voyage. What did you learn? How did it feel to make a difference? Sharing your experiences can inspire others to start their own giving project.

And why stop there? Share your story beyond just your crew. With permission, you might talk about your project in class, write a short story or draw a comic strip about it, and share it with your school or community. Your adventure could be the spark that lights a fire of generosity in others.

Remember, every great adventurer faces challenges, and it's okay if things didn't go exactly as planned. The important part is that you tried, and you learned. Like any skill, giving and helping others get easier and more effective the more you do it.

Now, as we conclude our giving project journey, think about what's next. The end of one adventure is just the beginning of another. How can you continue to make a difference? Maybe you spotted another need during your project, or you have a new idea that excites you. Let that be the starting point for your next mission of kindness.

Lastly, always remember the power of gratitude. Say thank you to everyone who helped you on your giving journey, including yourself. It takes a big heart to want to make the world a better place, and you should be proud of the steps you've taken, no matter how big or small.

So, brave adventurers, as we close the book on this chapter, remember that the story of your generosity is just beginning. The paths you choose to walk, the hands you extend in kindness, and the hearts you touch will write the most beautiful tales. And who knows? The lives you change the most might just be your own.

Wishing you many more adventures in giving, full of joy, learning, and plenty of fun. Remember, in the grand adventure of life, sharing with others isn't just a chapter—it's the theme that makes the whole story worth reading.

Now, go out there and make some magic happen, in your own unique way. The world is waiting for your special touch. Happy giving!

Chapter 6: Earning Your Own Money

Picture this: you've come up with the coolest idea for your very own business—maybe it's a lemonade stand, a pet-walking service, or perhaps creating and selling homemade bracelets. The thrill of turning your idea into reality is just the beginning. In this chapter, we're embarking on an adventure to discover how you can earn your own money. It's not just about pocket money; it's about setting sails towards independence and learning the value of hard work and creativity. Imagine the sense of pride and accomplishment you'll feel when you hold your first earnings in your hand, knowing you earned every cent on your own. We'll explore some smart and fun ways to get your entrepreneurial spirit fired up. Whether it's crafting a mini business plan that could rival the greatest adventurers in business or setting clear, achievable financial goals that light up your path like stars in the night sky, you're about to learn that earning your own money can open the door to a world of possibilities. So, grab your map and let's set off on this exciting journey together, discovering the treasures of earning and the endless adventures that money can bring into our lives.

Creative Ways to Earn

In the sprawling garden of life, finding unique ways to earn your own money can be one of the most thrilling adventures. Imagine transforming everyday skills and hobbies into your very own gold coins. Picture this: you're an artist at heart, and your drawings could brighten someone's day - why not sell your artwork? Or perhaps you have a green thumb, allowing you to sell plants or even help neighbors beautify their gardens. Don't forget the digital world - it's filled with opportunities, from creating online tutorials to showcasing your gaming skills. With each endeavor, you're not just earning money; you're embarking on a quest, discovering what you love to do and how you can share that gift with the world. The journey doesn't stop at making money; it's about growing, learning, and sailing towards your dreams on a ship you've built from the ground up. So grab your map and your compass; let's set sail into a sea of possibilities where your creativity and passion are the winds that drive your sails.

Activity: Your Mini Business Plan Imagine you're embarking on a grand adventure, one where you're the captain of your ship, steering toward the wide blue yonder. Only, in this adventure, your ship is a mini business, and the vast ocean is the bustling marketplace. Every captain needs a map, and that's precisely what a business plan is—a treasure map to success. So let's draw one together.

First, think about what you love doing. Do you enjoy making bracelets, baking cookies, or setting up lemonade stands? Your business should be something you're excited about because when you do what you love, it hardly feels like work. Imagine you're planting a seed of your favorite fruit; you'll tend it more lovingly knowing the sweet harvest ahead.

Now, every plan needs a name, something that shouts "This is me!" It's like naming your ship before it sails. What will you call your business? Make it catchy, make it shine, and most importantly, make it yours. It's the banner that flaps high on your ship, seen from afar.

With your ship named, you must next plot your course. Who will enjoy your treasures? Friends, family, neighbors? Or maybe there's a local market craving what you offer. Identifying who wants your goods is like finding islands teeming with gold. These people are your customers, and understanding what they love and need is key.

Even the finest captains can't sail alone. You might need a crew. Is this a solo journey, or will you recruit mates? Perhaps a friend with a knack for art could help design your signs, or a sibling could be your first mate, helping manage your booty. Decide who, if anyone, is joining your voyage.

Every successful expedition needs supplies. Whether it's the flour for your cookies or the beads for your bracelets, make a list. This part of your plan tells you what you need before setting sail, ensuring you're not stranded without essentials. It's okay to start small; even the grandest ships were once merely plans on paper.

Next, consider your treasure chest. Start-up costs are the gold coins you need upfront to embark on your journey. How much will your supplies cost? Remember, investing a bit of your own treasure now can lead to vast riches later. It's like buying the best maps and compasses, ensuring your journey's success.

Speaking of treasure, how will you price your bounty? It has to be a fair trade—the gold for your goods. Research what others charge for similar treasures. Not too high that it scares away the adventurous souls, and not too low that it doesn't reflect the sweat and love poured into your creation.

Your map is taking shape, but a vital part remains—the promotion of your voyage. How will you let the world know about your grand adventure? Maybe you'll craft signs as bright as lighthouses or tell tales of your wares so engaging that they spread like sea shanties from one end of the land to the other.

With your plan almost complete, it's crucial to think about the sea itself. Every marketplace has its storms and calm seas. Reflect on the challenges you might face. Perhaps it's other captains vying for the same treasure or unpredictable weather dampening your sales. How will you navigate these waters?

The best adventurers learn and adapt. As you embark on your journey, keep a logbook. Note what works and what doesn't, the winds that favor your sails, and those that don't. This log will be your guide, helping refine your map, making your next venture even more successful.

Before you set sail, remember why you started this voyage. It wasn't just for the gold, but for the thrill of the adventure, the joy of creating, and the pride of navigating your course. Success isn't just a chest full of coins; it's about the smiles, the learning, and the experiences gained.

Now, look at your plan, your map. It's more than just paper and ink; it's your dream charted out, a promise of adventures to come. Feel the wind in your sails, the horizon beckoning. With your mini business plan in hand, you're not just dreaming of distant lands—you're ready to explore them.

Remember, every great entrepreneur started somewhere, with a dream and a plan. Your journey begins now, with this map, your courage, and your creativity. Set your sights on the stars, young captain. The sea of business awaits, full of mysteries to unravel, lands to explore, and treasures to discover. Bon voyage!

Let this activity be more than just an exercise; let it be the start of something magical. Who knows what lands you'll discover, what people you'll meet, or what treasures you'll uncover? The world is vast, and your potential is limitless. So grab your pen, chart your course, and let the adventure unfold.

Setting Financial Goals

Imagine you're on a grand adventure through a mystical forest, your pockets jingling with golden coins you've earned from your lemonade stand. Up ahead, you see a bridge, but it doesn't lead just anywhere—it leads to your biggest dreams. Now, how do you cross it? That's where setting financial goals comes into play. Think of goals like magic keys that unlock the path to your dreams. Whether it's buying a new video game, saving for a bike, or even giving back to the community, knowing what you want is the first step. Once you set your mind on something special, you can start planning how to get there. Break it down into small steps, like saving a little every week from your allowance or the money you make from extra chores. But remember, it's not just about reaching the end; it's about enjoying the adventure along the way. Every saved penny and every smart spending choice gets you closer to your dream, turning you into a true money wizard in your own epic story.

Activity: Goal-Setting Workshop with Max In the heart of Max's Money World, where the trees were made of shimmering green dollars and the rivers flowed with sparkling coins, Max guided a group of eager young minds into a cozy, sunlit clearing. Today, they were embarking on an adventure unlike any other—a journey into the future, but armed with goals and the blueprint to reach them.

"Welcome, my young explorers," Max began, his voice warm and inviting. "Today, we'll chart the paths to our dreams. But remember, goals are like treasure maps; they guide us to the X that marks the spot." The children, with eyes wide and filled with wonder, nodded. They could almost see the treasure chests waiting for them at the end of their quests.

Max unfurled a giant scroll, its edges decorated with fascinating symbols and letters. "This," he announced, "is our canvas for the day." The children gathered around, eager to add their marks to the parchment. "First, let's dream. Close your eyes and think of something you wish to achieve. Big or small, let your heart decide."

As the gentle wind danced through the clearing, the children delved into their imaginations. Dreams of building the tallest skyscraper, mastering the art of painting, or sailing around the world on a boat made of recycled bottles filled their minds. One by one, they shared their dreams with Max, who listed them on the scroll with a feathered quill.

"Now," Max transitioned their attention, "behind every dream lies a goal—the stepping stones across the river of challenges." With a flick of his wand, Max materialized a ladder in the middle of the clearing. "Think of each rung as a goal, a step closer to your dream."

The lesson unfolded as they learned the importance of setting SMART goals—specific, measurable, attainable, relevant, and time-bound. Max explained how a wish like owning a bike becomes a goal when you plan to save $5 from your allowance each week for a year. Suddenly, the children's dreams felt within reach, not just far-off wishes.

"Setting a goal is like planting a seed," Max continued, now guiding them to a garden filled with all sorts of plants. "With care, patience, and a bit of sunshine and water, it grows over time into something wonderful." Each child planted a seed in this magical garden, symbolizing their commitment to their goals. They made a pledge to nurture their dreams just as they would care for their seeds.

To solidify their understanding, Max introduced them to the Goal Tracker—a magical tool that would help them keep an eye on their progress. Using a simple piece of parchment, they drew timelines and sketched mini milestones to celebrate along the way. Laughter and excitement filled the air as the children imagined reaching each milestone.

But Max reminded them, "On this journey, there will be obstacles. You might stumble or fall. Yet remember, every adventurer faces challenges. It's rising after the fall that makes you a true explorer."

Inspired by Max's words, the children fashioned shields from the leaves of the knowledge tree, each shield representing their resilience and determination. They understood that setbacks were part of the journey and promised to support one another.

As the sun began to set, painting the sky in hues of gold and pink, Max gathered the children for one last activity. "Dreams and goals love company," he said, sparking a flame of unity among them. "Share your dream with a friend, and let's promise to be each others' cheerleaders." Bonds formed in that moment, forged in the fire of shared aspirations and mutual support.

The workshop culminated in a ceremony where each child received a medal of courage, a token to remind them of the strength within. Max's sage advice, "Carry this as a reminder that your goals are valid and attainable, and you have the courage to achieve them," resonated deeply.

As the first star appeared in the twilight sky, Max concluded, "This is just the beginning of your journey. Keep dreaming, keep planning, and keep progressing. Remember, the treasure lies not just at the end but in the adventure itself."

The children left the clearing that evening, not just with dreams but with goals, a plan, and a community. They had learned that goal-setting wasn't just about reaching a destination but understanding and appreciating the journey. And as they disappeared into the horizon, their laughter and chatter blending with the evening choir of the forest, it was clear—they were ready to pursue their dreams, one goal at a time.

And so, the workshop with Max taught them that dreams are the seeds of reality, goals the sunlight and water that nurture them, and resilience and community the soil in which they flourish. With these lessons etched in their hearts, the children were equipped not just for financial success but for a life of purpose and passion.

Chapter 7: Borrowing and Lending

Imagine you're setting off on a grand adventure, but instead of packing a backpack, you're gathering tools for your financial future. In this chapter, we'll embark on a journey through the world of borrowing and lending. Think of it like a trek through a mystical forest where every tree is an opportunity and every stone, a lesson to learn. Borrowing might seem like a magic spell that grants you money when you need it, but it's really more like a promise—a promise you make to return what was lent to you, often with a little extra as a thank-you, known as interest. It's like borrowing a neighbor's shovel to build a sandcastle and returning it with a slice of your grandpa's famous apple pie. We'll discover why it's super important to keep your promises, especially when money is involved. Not only does it help you build trust, but it also turns you into a lending and borrowing wizard, mastering the art of making and managing these money moves with confidence. As we navigate through the enchanting paths of borrowing responsibly and understanding the importance of repaying, imagine planting seeds of trust and responsibility that grow into towering trees of credibility and financial stability. So, let's grab our imaginary shovels (and maybe a slice of pie for the road) and dig into the essential lessons of borrowing and lending!

The Basics of Borrowing

Imagine you're on a grand adventure through a mystical forest, and you stumble upon a lantern that grants wishes—but there's a twist. You can wish for anything, but you must promise to give something of equal value back in the future. This is a lot like borrowing! When you borrow, you get something now, like money or a video game from a friend, with the promise that you'll return it later or pay back with something else of value. It lightens your backpack on your journey for a while, letting you sprint ahead or climb higher with less weighing you down. But remember, returning what you borrowed keeps the paths open for your next adventure, and shows you're someone who can be trusted with even bigger and more thrilling quests. So, as you trek through your financial forest, think about borrowing as a tool that can help you explore further, as long as you respect the promise to return what was lent to you. It's like having a magical accessory in your explorer's kit, useful and powerful, but only with the right intentions and the honor to uphold your word.

Activity: The Family Bank Loan Simulation

Imagine you're part of a grand adventure, not through dense forests or across the high seas, but right within the walls of your own home. This journey involves you, your family, and a quest to understand how banks and loans work in the real world. It's a thrilling simulation called "The Family Bank Loan Simulation".

In this activity, your home transforms into a bustling bank. Someone will be the banker (maybe mom, dad, or an older sibling), and the others will become customers. As a customer, you have big dreams, maybe buying a beautiful bike or investing in a small lemonade stand – but you need a loan to make this dream come true. This is where the family bank comes into play.

The banker will give you an initial amount of play money. This money represents your loan. But don't forget, just like in real life, this money isn't free. It comes with an interest rate. Interest is a bit like a rental fee - it's the extra money you pay back for borrowing money.

Next, you'll decide what your loan is for and how you plan to make money to pay it back. Will you do extra chores? Maybe create and sell some artwork? It's your call, but make it realistic. The goal is not just to dream big but also to plan meticulously.

Over the next week, you'll work on your project, keeping track of your earnings. This part of the quest requires dedication and hard work, but remember, every great adventurer needs to overcome obstacles to reach their treasure. Your treasure in this case is the satisfaction of paying back your loan and earning a profit.

Halfway through the week, the banker will check in. This is a great time to discuss your progress. Are you on track, or do you need to adjust your plan? This meeting is crucial because it simulates real-life financial reviews that happen in the world of adults.

At the end of the week, it's time to settle up. You'll calculate how much you owe with interest and pay the bank back. If you've planned well and worked hard, you'll have enough to cover your loan and then some. This leftover money is your profit – your reward for a job well done.

This activity doesn't just end here. It's a chance for a family discussion. Talk about what worked, what didn't, and what it felt like to borrow money. Did earning the money to pay back the loan feel different than just receiving an allowance or gift?

For the banker, it's also a revealing journey. Managing a bank (even a pretend one) involves responsibility and decision-making. It's about assessing risk - deciding who is likely to pay the loan back, and under what conditions a loan is a good idea.

Through "The Family Bank Loan Simulation", you learn the importance of responsible borrowing and lending. It teaches fiscal discipline, the value of hard work, and the satisfaction that comes from reaching financial goals.

The story doesn't end when the simulation does. Carry these lessons with you. Whether you're saving for something small or have big dreams for the future, understanding the principles of borrowing and lending, interest, and repayment is invaluable.

Remember, the journey of financial education is ongoing. There will be more adventures, more challenges, and more lessons. But with each step, you become more careful, confident, and capable in managing your money.

"The Family Bank Loan Simulation" is not just a make-believe adventure. It's preparing you for real-life quests, where the stakes are real, and the rewards are meaningful. It's teaching you not just to be a dreamer, but a doer, who knows how to turn visions into reality through smart financial planning and hard work.

So, as you move forward in your journey of financial wisdom, look back on this experience as a valuable chapter. You've not merely played a game; you've practiced life skills that will guide you through the world of finance, helping you navigate your way to personal prosperity and success.

And remember, in the grand adventure of life, you're the hero of your own story. Financial knowledge is one of the most powerful tools in your arsenal. Use it wisely, and there's no limit to the heights you can reach. Let's embark on this journey with courage, determination, and a spirit of adventure.

The Importance of Paying Back

Imagine you're on a grand adventure through a mystical forest, full of twisting paths and hidden treasures. Along the way, a kind squirrel lends you a golden acorn to help you in your quest. Now, think how important it is to return this golden acorn once your journey is complete. In the world outside the forest, borrowing and lending might not involve golden acorns, but the principle remains the same. When someone—a friend, a family member, or even a bank—trusts you enough to lend you something, whether it's a few dollars to buy a snack or a larger sum to kick-start a lemonade stand, paying them back is just as crucial. It's like planting a seed of trust that can grow into a mighty tree, showing that you're thankful and respect the faith they've placed in you. More importantly, it ensures that they'll be there for you on your next adventure, ready to lend a hand—or an acorn—once again. So, as we navigate through our financial forests, let's not forget the significance of returning what we've borrowed, nurturing our paths with the seeds of reliability and gratitude.

Activity: The Trust Game Continuing on our adventure into the world of finance, we stumble upon a very important concept: trust. In the realm of borrowing and lending, trust plays a huge role. Imagine, if you will, a game that can illuminate the essence of trust in such transactions. Welcome to the Trust Game, an activity designed to teach you the value of trustworthiness and the repercussions of not adhering to agreements.

Let's set the scene for our game. Picture two friends, let's call them Alex and Jamie. Alex needs some money to buy a new book they have been wanting to read but doesn't have enough money at the moment. Jamie offers to lend Alex the money, trusting that Alex will pay it back as promised. This is where our game begins.

To play the Trust Game, you'll need at least two players. If you have more, that's even better; you can pair off or take turns being the borrower and lender. The aim of the game is to understand what it feels like to be in both positions, to learn the value of keeping your word, and to see what happens when you don't.

In the first round, one player will lend a small, inconsequential item to the other, something like a pencil or a piece of candy, with the promise that it will be returned after a short period, say by the end of the day. The lender must trust the borrower, and the borrower must keep their word. If the borrower returns the item as promised, the lender's trust grows. If not, the lender's trust diminishes.

After the first round, discuss how it felt to trust someone with something that belonged to you. Then, flip the roles and play again. Notice any differences in how you feel when you are the one borrowing from someone else.

Now, escalate the game slightly. This time, the item to be lent should be slightly more valuable, maybe a favorite book or a video game. This increases the stakes and tests the trust even further. Remember, the goal isn't to upset anyone but to understand the dynamics of trust deeply.

Through these rounds, players will start to notice a pattern. When trust is honored, relationships strengthen. But when trust is broken, doubt creeps in. It's much like how banks decide to whom they will lend money. They must trust that the person will pay them back, or they take a risk in losing that money.

Consider bringing the game to a close by gathering all participants and reflecting on the experiences shared. Ask questions like: How did it feel to have someone trust you? What went through your mind when you had to trust someone else? How did it feel when someone broke your trust, and how hard was it to rebuild that trust?

For an added layer, talk about consequences in the real world when trust is broken in financial matters. Explain how failing to repay a loan can affect someone's ability to borrow in the future, deflate their credit score, and narrow their opportunities.

Conclude the Trust Game by underscoring the significance of trust, not just in financial matters but in life. Honoring promises and commitments is a cornerstone of integrity and character. Now, challenge each participant to be extra mindful of their promises and commitments for the next week, noting how it affects their relationships and self-esteem.

The Trust Game is not just a game; it's a journey into understanding the fundamental human value of trust. Like a delicate plant, trust must be nurtured and cared for. In the world of finance, this translates to being reliable and disciplined with money, especially when it involves others. Building a good reputation for trustworthiness can open doors to greater financial opportunities and stronger relationships.

Let this game be a stepping stone towards learning how to manage money wisely and understanding the deep impact our actions have on our financial futures and the relationships we cherish. Just like Alex and Jamie, learning to trust and be trustworthy with money is a valuable lesson that will serve you well throughout your life.

Remember, in the grand adventure of life, being trustworthy is akin to being a treasure chest filled with gold. It makes you valuable not just in your financial dealings but in your personal relationships and your journey towards becoming a reliable, valued member of society. So, take the lessons from the Trust Game to heart, and let them guide you as you navigate the exciting world of finance and beyond.

Chapter 8: Protecting Your Money

Imagine you're on an adventure, searching for hidden treasures. Your treasure isn't gold or jewels; it's the money you've been saving bit by bit. But, just like in any good adventure, there are dragons to slay – or, in our case, risks to protect our money from. It's not just about locking your treasure chest; it's about being smart both online and offline. Have you ever heard of the term "cyber-smart"? Think of it as knowing the right spells to protect your treasure from digital dragons that lurk on the internet, trying to trick you into giving them access to your cash. And just like in any quest, sometimes we might stumble or make a mistake, like spending our money on something we don't really need, or forgetting to keep our money safe. But fear not! Every mistake is a lesson learned on how to be a better guardian of your treasure. So, let's dive into the secrets of keeping your money safe, outsmarting those digital dragons, and ensuring that your treasure grows. It's all about being a brave, smart guardian of your money, ready to face any challenge with wisdom and courage.

Being Money Smart Online

In a world where everything from games to pocket money can hop online, it's crucial to be a guardian of your digital dimes. Think of the internet as a vast forest, one where adventure awaits but so do tricky foxes, ready to swipe your snacks if you're not careful. You wouldn't leave your piggy bank open in the park, would you? Imagine your online money is like a treasure chest. To keep it safe, you need to know where the traps are hidden. Phishing scams, sneaky subscriptions, or too-good-to-be-true offers are like the tangled vines that can trip you up and snatch your gold coins right from under your nose. But fear not! You've got the map to navigate this forest, armed with knowledge and a keen eye, you can dodge the traps and keep your treasure safe. Securing your loot online isn't just smart; it's like being the hero in your own story, outwitting the villains and protecting the kingdom's riches - your future self will thank you for being such a savvy guardian!

Activity: Cyber Smart Quiz Just like a knight needs armor to protect themselves from dragons, you need to be cyber smart to protect your treasure from internet trolls and scams. Let's embark on a grand adventure into the land of the internet, where being smart with your money isn't just wise, it's essential. Are you ready to test your knowledge and see if you can be a Cyber Smart champion?

In a world that's more connected than ever, your journey starts here. Imagine stepping into a vast digital kingdom, where each click can lead you to wondrous treasures or hidden traps. This quiz is your map, helping you navigate through the cyber wilderness with skill and wisdom.

Before we dive into the questions, remember, the internet is a double-edged sword. It's filled with incredible resources for learning and fun, but also dangers that lurk under the guise of tempting offers and urgent warnings. Like any true adventurer, your greatest weapon is your knowledge.

Our first question tests your ability to identify a scam. You receive an email from a prince claiming he will share his kingdom's riches if you just send your bank account details. What do you do? A) Send the information because, hey, who doesn't want to be rich? B) Ignore and delete the email, knowing that true princes don't wander the internet looking for helpers.

The correct answer is B. Real life isn't a fairytale. These scams prey on our desires for a fantastical windfall but remember, when something sounds too good to be true, it usually is.

Next, let's explore the realm of passwords. What makes a strong password? A) Your birthday or pet's name because it's easy to remember, or B) A mix of letters, numbers, and symbols that doesn't relate directly to your personal information. The correct choice is B. A formidable password is like a dragon's scales—hard to break through, protecting your precious information inside.

Here comes a trickier challenge. You find a website offering free video games, but it asks for your credit card information to sign up. Do you A) Enter the details because free games are worth it, or B) Search for reviews of the site first and opt not to provide your credit card for free content? The wise decision is B. Always question why a free service needs your payment information. A cautious adventurer lives to quest another day.

Imagine you're navigating through a bustling marketplace, the internet's version of a shopping district. You see an ad for an amazing product at an unbelievably low price. Is this a red flag? Yes, it often is. Just like in the real world, if a deal seems too incredible, it might be a merchant's trick to lure you into a trap.

Now, let's talk about sharing personal information online. Think of your personal info as the keys to your kingdom. Would you give these keys to a stranger you met in the cyber streets? Protecting your personal information is paramount. Always ensure you're on a secure and trusted site (look for the lock icon in the web address) before sharing any details.

Adventurer, how do you respond if you accidentally click on something suspicious? A) Panic and abandon your quest, or B) Calmly close the window and tell a trusted adult about the mistake? The courageous choice is B. Everyone makes mistakes, but the brave learn from them and seek help when needed.

Do you download apps or games from the internet? If so, making sure they come from trusted sources protects you from invisible monsters like viruses and malware. Always download from official app stores or websites, ensuring your digital steed is shielded from harm.

Engaging in the online realm also means being kind and respectful. The golden rule? Treat others how you wish to be treated, whether in a castle, a forest, or the vast online world. Cyberbullying is a dragon that we all must vow to fight against.

As the sunset colors the digital kingdom's skyline, reflecting on today's journey reminds us of the many paths we navigate. Being cyber smart is not just about avoiding pitfalls; it's about journeying through the internet with awareness, respect, and courage.

You've reached the end of the Cyber Smart Quiz, a testament to your valor and wisdom in protecting your treasure. Armed with knowledge, you're more prepared to face the challenges and wonders of the digital world. May your adventures be many, your battles honorable, and your treasures protected.

Remember, young adventurer, the internet holds many keys to knowledge and discovery. Use it wisely, protect your personal kingdom fiercely, and always be curious. For in curiosity lies the true treasure of learning and growth.

In closing, let this quiz not be the end but a beginning. A start of your journey to becoming not just cyber smart, but a true protector of your domain in the vast, ever-expanding digital universe. Your quest has just begun, and the paths you choose will lead to stories yet to be told.

May your light shine bright, and your cyber journeys always bring you back home safely. Until our next adventure, keep your wits sharp and your passwords secure.

Avoiding Money Mistakes

In the grand quest to protect our coins and conquer chaos in our financial kingdom, let's embark on an adventure through the mystical realm of Avoiding Money Mistakes. Picture yourself as a brave knight, with your shield of knowledge and sword of savvy decisions, battling the dragons of debt and the trolls of impulsive buying. Imagine discovering a treasure chest, not filled with gold, but with golden tips to keep your money safe and sound. It's like being a superhero, where instead of fighting crime, you're battling against making those slip-ups that could see your hard-earned money disappearing like magic. By becoming a master in recognizing those sneaky traps and temptations, you're not just saving your money; you're setting up a fortress around it. This quest requires sharp eyes, a steady heart, and the wisdom to know that every choice you make builds the path to your fabled land of financial security. So let's sharpen our wits and ready our resolve as we step forth into a world brimming with potential pitfalls, armed with the secret maps and enchanted strategies that will guide us to victory in the timeless tale of protecting our precious pennies.

Activity: Spot the Scam with Max Once upon a sunny afternoon, in the heart of Moneyville, a small town known for its wise and wealthy residents, Max the Money Mogul decided it was time for a new adventure. This wasn't going to be just any adventure, though. It was one that would require the sharp eyes and keen minds of the town's youngest residents. "Today," Max declared with a twinkle in his eye, "we're going to become scam detectives!"

The children of Moneyville gathered around, intrigued by the challenge. Max explained that the world, even a place as lovely as Moneyville, had its share of tricksters trying to fool people into giving away their hard-earned money. He unfolded a colorful board game dotted with illustrations of various scenarios, each one representing a potential scam. "Your mission," Max said, pointing to the game, "is to spot which ones are scams and explain why. Think you can do it?"

The game began, and the children huddled in groups, whispering and pointing at the board. One picture showed a person winning an online contest they never entered, another depicted an unbelievable offer for a free vacation—each scenario slightly more enticing than the last. Max strolled around, overhearing their discussions, nodding in approval at their skepticism and guiding them gently when they were unsure.

"Remember," Max reminded them, "if something sounds too good to be true, it probably is." This became the mantra of the day, as groups moved their pieces around the board, identifying suspicious offers with surprising accuracy. They learned about phishing emails, fake charity donations, and too-good-to-be-true investment opportunities.

As the game progressed, it wasn't just about spotting scams anymore. The children began to understand the value of questioning and the importance of protecting their personal information. "Why would someone need my social security number to send me a prize?" one child pondered aloud, echoing a newfound understanding that would serve her well beyond the game.

Max was impressed. Not only were the kids getting better at identifying scams, but they were also learning the reasons behind them. "Scammers prey on our desire for easy rewards," he explained, "but remember, earning money takes effort and smarts. Just like you're all showing today."

Suddenly, a scam scenario popped up that stumped everyone. It was an offer for a mystery shopper job that required the applicant to pay for a "certification fee" upfront. The room went quiet as the young detectives deliberated. "What do you think, Max?" one of the children finally asked.

"Ah, a tricky one indeed," Max said, smiling. "Let's break it down together." They discussed how legitimate job offers shouldn't require payment to get started and how important it was to research a company before agreeing to anything. This revelation was a lightbulb moment for many of the kids.

The game concluded with laughter and cheers as Max crowned the children "Chief Scam Detectors of Moneyville." They had spotted all the scams, and more importantly, they understood why they were scams. "You've all done an amazing job today," Max beamed. "You're proof that being smart with money isn't just about saving and spending wisely—it's also about protecting it."

To celebrate, Max handed out certificates of achievement to each child, promising them that the skills they learned today were just the beginning of their financial education journey. "Remember, my young detectives, in a world full of scams, your knowledge is your power and your skepticism, a shield. Use them well."

As the sun began to set over Moneyville, the children gathered their certificates and chattered excitedly about their newfound roles as scam detectors. They had embarked on this adventure full of curiosity and emerged with wisdom far beyond their years.

In the days that followed, tales of the scam-spotting adventure spread throughout Moneyville, inspiring others to be more cautious and informed. Parents and children alike started having conversations about safe financial practices, and the local schools decided to incorporate similar activities into their curriculums.

Max watched all of this unfold with a sense of pride and accomplishment. He had set out to educate the children of Moneyville in a fun and engaging way, but he ended up sparking a movement—a community-wide commitment to financial literacy and scam awareness.

The "Activity: Spot the Scam with Max" wasn't just a game; it was a stepping stone towards a more informed and financially savvy generation. And as Max often mused, sitting on his porch looking out over the town, that was the true treasure at the end of this adventure.

So, the next time you come across an offer that seems too good to be true, remember the lessons from Moneyville. Ask questions, do your research, and never underestimate the power of a skeptical mind. After all, in the quest for financial wisdom, every scam spotted is a lesson learned and a disaster averted.

Chapter 9: Fun with Numbers

Imagine embarking on a treasure hunt, where the maps are your personal budgets and the treasures are your financial goals. In "Fun with Numbers," we dive into the world of making a personal budget and understanding prices and sales, turning what might seem like boring tasks into an exciting adventure. Just like a ship captain navigating through the vast seas, you'll learn how to steer your money ship with the help of your budget map, making sure you have enough supplies (savings) to reach your destinations (goals) without getting lost. And what's an adventure without a bit of challenge? The Discount Dash will have you racing against time, applying your newfound knowledge of percentages and sales to snag the best deals, teaching you how to stretch your dollars further. This chapter isn't just about crunching numbers; it's about discovering the power and freedom that comes from understanding and controlling your finances. You'll start seeing numbers as allies in your quest for financial wisdom, turning every price tag and budget line into a puzzle piece of your bigger financial picture.

Making a Personal Budget

Imagine your favorite video game, where you're on an epic quest through uncharted territories, each decision shaping the adventure ahead. In real life, making a personal budget is kind of like mapping out your quest, ensuring you have enough supplies (in this case, money) to complete each level (or month) successfully. A budget isn't just a boring list of numbers; it's your magical scroll guiding you through the challenges of saving and spending wisely. You start by jotting down the gold coins (money) you earn, like allowances or birthday money. Then, you track the coins you spend, maybe on video games, snacks, or saving for something big like a bike. The real trick is making sure you don't run out of coins before the month is over. It's about making choices, like a hero deciding which path to take to save the kingdom. Do you spend your coins on a new game now or save them so you can buy something even cooler later? By keeping a budget, you're the master of your own financial quest, learning to balance your treasure chest so you're prepared for any adventure that comes your way.

Activity: Max's Monthly Budget Challenge

In the world of adventure, where every twist and turn brings a new discovery, there lived a curious chap named Max. Max wasn't your ordinary adventurer; he was a Money Mogul on a mission to teach the young minds the magic of managing money. Today, Max has thrown down the gauntlet with a challenge that's both fun and filled with learning - the Monthly Budget Challenge.

Before we dive into the challenge, let's remind ourselves what a budget is. Imagine you have a treasure chest, but instead of gold and jewels, it's filled with something even more valuable: your money. A budget is a map that shows you how to use this treasure wisely, so you have enough for everything you need and even some of what you want.

Max's Monthly Budget Challenge kicks off with a simple task: tracking your money. For a whole month, Max wants you to jot down every penny that comes into your little treasure chest, be it from allowances, birthday money, or finding a dollar on the sidewalk. And don't forget to note where your money goes! Whether you're spending it on comics, saving for a new video game, or giving some to charity, Max says it's important to keep a record.

Why do you ask? Well, just like a ship's captain needs to know where his ship is heading, you need to know where your money is going. It helps you make smarter decisions, like finding ways to save more or deciding if you really need to buy that new toy.

After you've tracked your money for a month, it's time to make your very own budget. Max has a simple formula: Income - Savings = Expenses. First, add up all the money you received during the month. This is your income. Then, decide how much of that you want to save. Whatever's left after saving is what you can spend. This is your expense limit.

Now, here's where the challenge gets exciting. With the budget you've just created, Max wants you to plan the next month. Think about the things you need to spend money on and the things you want. Remember, the goal is to not spend more than your expense limit.

Max has a special tip: always set aside a little for surprises or unplanned expenses. Maybe your friend invites you to go to the movies, or you need a new notebook for school. Having a "just in case" fund means you won't be caught off guard.

If you find yourself spending too much in one area, Max encourages you to get creative. Maybe you can walk to your friend's house instead of taking the bus, or swap books and games with buddies instead of buying new ones. There are tons of ways to stretch your expense limit without feeling like you're missing out.

For those of you who love a bit of competition, Max suggests turning the budget challenge into a game with your friends or family. See who can save the most or who can come up with the cleverest ways to stay within their budget. It's not just about winning, though; sharing ideas and learning together makes everyone a champion in Max's eyes.

At the end of the second month, sit down and review how you did. Were you able to stick to your budget? Did you find some areas where you could cut back? Or maybe you discovered you had more room for savings than you thought. Reflecting on these questions helps you understand your spending habits better and gives you a chance to celebrate your successes.

Max knows that talking about money can sometimes feel a bit daunting. But he believes that by tackling it head-on with activities like the Monthly Budget Challenge, you're not just learning to manage money; you're also building confidence in your ability to make decisions and take control of your financial future.

Beyond just numbers and budgets, Max wants you to remember that money is a tool. It's something that can help you achieve your dreams, whether that's buying a new bicycle, helping out a friend in need, or saving for a college education. By mastering money management now, you're setting sail towards a future filled with possibilities.

As you wrap up the Monthly Budget Challenge, Max encourages you to keep the adventure going. Maybe you can experiment with different savings goals or explore more creative ways to earn money. The journey to becoming a Money Mogul is an ongoing one, full of learning, growth, and, most importantly, fun.

Max's final piece of advice? Always stay curious and keep exploring. Just like the greatest adventurers and explorers, with a map (your budget) in hand and a keen eye for discovery, there's no telling what treasures you'll find on your financial journey. The Monthly Budget Challenge is just the beginning. Who knows what other adventures lie ahead?

Understanding Prices and Sales

Have you ever wondered why the same toy can have different prices at two stores? Or why things go on sale just when you've saved enough allowance to pay full price? It's like a treasure hunt where prices dance and sales pop up like magic! Imagine embarking on an adventure to discover how prices change and why sales happen. It's a world where numbers tell stories and every tag holds secrets waiting to be unveiled. By diving into the mysteries of prices and sales, you'll not only become a savvy shopper but also a smart saver. You'll learn how to spot true bargains, understand when it's best to wait for a sale, and even predict when your favorite items might cost less. This journey isn't just about saving a few pennies—it's about equipping yourself with knowledge that turns you into a financial wizard, capable of making your money stretch further than you ever imagined. So, let's set off on this quest together, exploring the exciting world of prices and sales, where every discovery empowers you to make wise choices with your hard-earned cash.

Activity: The Discount Dash Imagine you're in a race, but instead of running on a track, you're dashing through the aisles of your favorite store. Your mission? To snag the most incredible deals ever seen! This isn't just any race; it's the Discount Dash, a thrilling adventure where your wits and knowledge of percentages turn into savings!

First things first, every great adventurer needs to know what they're searching for. In the world of shopping, that means understanding sales signs. Imagine you see a sign that says "25% off." What does that mean? Put simply, the store is offering to take off 25 out of every 100 parts of the price, making items more affordable. It's like the store is giving you a portion of the price back as a gift!

Now, let's add a bit of strategy to our dash. When two signs catch your eye—one saying "30% off" and another "Buy One Get One 50% off"—which do you choose? This choice might seem puzzling, but with a dash of math, the answer can be found. Calculate the savings each option offers, and like a true discount detective, choose the one that gives you the most bang for your buck.

Before we dive deeper into the discounts, remember, the goal isn't just to buy as much as you can. Imagine you're on a treasure hunt; the real victory comes from finding valuable treasures, not just any old thing. So, when you see a sale, ask yourself, "Do I really need this, or is the thrill of the discount swaying me?"

This exciting race also teaches an important lesson about patience. Sometimes, the best deal comes to those who wait. Maybe you've had your eye on a video game or a pair of sneakers. Instead of buying them on the spot, you wait, and bam, they go on sale. That's the satisfaction of a savvy saver!

In the midst of our dash, let's pause for a mini-challenge. Next time you're shopping with a grown-up, ask to see the receipt after checkout. See if you can spot how much was saved from discounts. It's like being a detective, uncovering the savings hidden in the long list of purchases.

Speaking of being smart with money, sometimes the store offers deals that aren't as grand as they seem. A sign might shout, "BIG SALE! UP TO 75% OFF!" But the key words are "up to." Not everything is 75% off; some items might only be a tiny bit cheaper. Keep your eyes peeled for the real deals.

Now, a true adventurer knows the importance of sharing their knowledge. After mastering the art of the dash, share what you've learned with a friend or a sibling. Teach them how to read discount signs and calculate savings. It's like passing on a treasure map for them to follow.

During your next Discount Dash, remember to be mindful of your budget. It's like your trusty backpack in our shopping adventure—too much weight (or spending) can slow you down. Make sure what you're picking up is worth the price and fits into your budget like a puzzle piece.

And what about online shopping? The Discount Dash isn't limited to physical stores. The internet is filled with digital deals waiting to be discovered. Use your newfound skills to hunt down promo codes and special offers. It's like unlocking a secret level in your favorite video game, where the rewards are discounts and savings.

Let's not forget the role of sales tax. It might not seem like much, but it adds up. When you're calculating a deal, remember to include tax to avoid any surprises. It's like accounting for all the twists and turns in a maze—planning ahead ensures you make it to the finish line without any hiccups.

As we near the end of our dash, reflect on the journey. Every race, every challenge, and every victory in finding the best deal has taught you valuable lessons about money management. It's not just about how fast you can go or how much you can buy; it's about making wise choices and understanding the value of a dollar.

For your final lap in the Discount Dash, set yourself a challenge. Next time you're out shopping, see if you can save a certain amount of money from discounts alone. Make it a game, and aim to beat your previous score. It's a fun way to put your skills to the test and see how much you've grown as a discount dasher.

In the end, remember that the Discount Dash is more than just a game or an activity. It's a journey toward becoming a smart spender and saver, skills that will guide you throughout life. Every discount discovered and every dollar saved brings you one step closer to your financial goals. So keep dashing, keep learning, and keep growing. The world of savings is vast and full of adventures waiting for you.

And with that, you've completed the Discount Dash. You've raced through the aisles, navigated through percentages, and emerged victorious with deals and knowledge in hand. You are now a seasoned discount detective, ready to take on your next financial adventure with confidence. Go forth and dash wisely!

Chapter 10: Money Around the World

Imagine embarking on a grand adventure across the globe, where every stop introduces you to a new kind of money magic. In "Money Around the World," we dive into the colorful world of currencies galore. From the towering skyscrapers of Tokyo where yen are spent, to the bustling markets of Cairo dealing in pounds, every country has its unique way of using money. It's like stepping into a treasure chest where dollars, euros, rupees, and pesos shine like gems. And just as exciting is discovering how kids like you save, spend, and think about their money in far-off lands. Through thrilling activities like the Currency Conversion Contest, you'll become a savvy currency converter. Meanwhile, the International Money Diary activity bridges oceans, letting you peek into the piggy banks and shopping carts of your global neighbors. This journey is more than just about becoming worldly wise—it's about understanding that no matter where we are, our dreams, goals, and the joy of responsibly managing money connect us all. So, let's set sail into the fascinating world of "Money Around the World," where the richness of our discoveries goes far beyond the coins and notes in our hands.

Currencies Galore

Imagine opening a treasure chest filled with shiny coins and crisp bills from all over the world. Each piece in that chest tells a story, a story of distant lands, cultures, and economies. This is what our chapter on "Currencies Galore" is all about. Every country has its own unique currency, like the colorful euros of Europe, the beautiful yen notes from Japan, or the intricately designed rupees from India. It's like each country has its own language of money, but instead of words, they use these fascinating currencies to communicate value. What's even more exciting is that the value of these currencies can change compared to others, making the world of money a dynamic and ever-evolving adventure. So, let's embark on this journey together, exploring the rich tapestry of world currencies, understanding what makes each one special, and perhaps, we'll even discover a bit more about the world itself along the way. It's not just about numbers and exchange rates; it's about opening our eyes to the diversity and richness of cultures around our globe through the lens of money.

Activity: Currency Conversion Contest Imagine you're about to embark on an adventure, not just any adventure, but one that will take you on a whirlwind trip around the globe, all from the comfort of your classroom or living room. You see, the world is a vast place, filled with countless cultures and, you guessed it, different types of money!

In this spirited contest, you and your friends will dive into the exciting world of currencies - money from different countries. You'll discover that in Japan, people buy things using yen, while in France, they use euros. It's like each country has its own unique language of money!

The challenge here is simple yet thrilling. You'll be given a list of items, from a slice of pizza in New York to a traditional lantern in Vietnam. Your mission is to convert the cost of these items from their local currency into US dollars, using currency conversion rates. Sounds like a real quest, doesn't it?

To kick things off, gather in teams or tackle this challenge solo. You'll need a currency conversion chart, which you can find online or in financial sections of newspapers. Make sure to use the most current rates because, just like the waves of the ocean, currency rates change daily.

Let's take an example to warm up. If a toy car costs 10 euros and the current conversion rate is 1 euro to 1.2 US dollars, how much does the toy car cost in US dollars? If you answered $12, you're right on the money!

As you embark on this journey, think of yourself as a globetrotter, hopping from country to country, learning not just about money, but about the culture and people behind it. Each currency tells a story, from the monuments pictured on coins and notes to the heroes celebrated.

Paying attention to details is key. Make sure to carefully note the conversion rates and calculate precisely. It's not just about winning; it's about embarking on a journey of discovery, understanding the value of different currencies, and how they play a crucial role in the global economy.

Once you've converted all the items on your list, compare your answers with your peers. This part is like unveiling a treasure chest of knowledge. You'll see how the cost of living varies around the world, sparking conversations about why that might be and what impacts these differences.

For accountability and a bit of extra fun, each team or individual will present their findings with a creative twist. You could create a mini travel brochure, a world map with currency symbols, or even a digital slideshow showcasing the items and their converted costs.

Remember, while this is a contest, the goal isn't just to win, but to embark on a learning adventure. It's about expanding your horizons, understanding the value of money in different settings, and becoming more globally aware.

As you tally up the scores, you'll find that some might have missed the mark while others hit the nail on the head. Don't fret if your conversions weren't perfect. This activity is a stepping stone, paving the way for you to become more financially savvy and culturally aware.

Reflect on this journey by discussing what surprised you the most. Was it the cost of a simple meal in another country? Or how much the currency conversion rates can affect how we perceive value? These reflections are like the compass that guides you through the financial world, helping you navigate with confidence.

As we wrap up this contest, remember that the world of money is vast and filled with mysteries waiting to be unraveled. Today, you've taken one step closer to understanding it, not just through numbers and rates, but through the stories and cultures intertwined with each currency.

So, hold onto this experience as you continue your adventure in financial education. Let it remind you that money, in all its forms, is more than just paper and coins; it's a passport to understanding the world and the diverse tapestry of people in it.

And who knows? Maybe one day, you'll find yourself using yen, euros, or pounds on your own adventures. Until then, keep exploring, keep learning, and most importantly, keep dreaming. For in the world of finance, as in life, the journey is just as important as the destination.

How Other Kids Save and Spend

Just like stars twinkling differently across the sky, kids around the world manage their money in fascinating ways that sparkle with ingenuity. Imagine trekking through the bustling streets of Tokyo, where children receive otoshidama, money gifts during New Year, teaching them the value of saving from an early age. Or, sail across to Italy, where a young heart might splurge on a gelato with coins clutched in a fist, learning the sweet balance between saving and spending. In the sandy dunes of Egypt, kids might be tucking away pounds to one day buy a beautiful hand-painted kite. Every corner of the globe offers unique stories of young savers and spenders, each narrative rich with lessons on patience, dreams, and the joy found in both saving for tomorrow and relishing the delights of today. From the piggy banks snug on shelves in Canada to the digital wallets buzzing in Australia's pockets, children are embarking on journeys, navigating the vast seas of financial wisdom with courage and curiosity, all the while crafting their tales of triumphs, mishaps, and discoveries in the art of managing money.

Activity: International Money Diary Imagine you're embarking on a grand adventure, spanning the corners of the earth, diving into the lives of kids all around the globe to discover how they save, spend, and view money in their daily lives. Think of it as your very own international mission, right from the comfort of your reading nook.

In this exercise, you will create an International Money Diary. This isn't just any diary; it will be a collection of stories, facts, and insights into how children from different parts of the world interact with money. Are you ready to be a global explorer?

First, let's pick countries. Consider choosing one from each continent to get a diverse view. How about Japan from Asia, Brazil from South America, Kenya from Africa, Canada from North America, Australia from Oceania, and Italy from Europe? Each of these places has its own unique money story to tell.

To start your diary, dedicate a page to each country. At the top, write the name of the country and draw or paste a picture of its currency. Did you know that Japan uses Yen, and Australia uses the Australian Dollar? Isn't it exciting to learn about these differences?

Next, for each country, try to find a story of a kid your age. What do they save their money for? How do they earn it? In Kenya, for example, a kid might save their money to buy books for school, while in Canada, perhaps they're saving for a new hockey stick. Capture these stories in your diary.

It's interesting to note how the value of chores and allowances differs. In Brazil, a child might earn money by helping around the house, similar to in the United States. But how much they earn can vary greatly. Write down what you find about chores and allowances in your diary.

Now, let's think about spending. In Italy, children might spend their money on gelato with friends. However, in Japan, they might save up for the latest manga or a new video game. Document these spending habits in your diary and think about what you like to save up for.

And what about saving? In Australia, many kids have a savings account that they deposit birthday or holiday money into. Does this sound like you, or is this a new idea? Explore and jot down these habits in your diary, making note of the similarities and differences.

Educational expenses are another aspect to consider. In some countries, kids save money to afford school uniforms or books. This highlights the importance and value they place on education. Record your findings and reflections in your diary.

As you journey through these countries in your diary, pay attention to the role of digital money. More and more kids are using apps or digital wallets to manage their finances. How common is this in the countries you're exploring? This might be an exciting area to dive into, seeing as digital money is becoming a big part of our financial lives.

After completing your diary entries, take a moment to reflect. What surprised you the most? Were there any habits or practices you'd like to adopt? This diary isn't just a collection of stories; it's a mirror reflecting a world of possibilities when it comes to managing money.

Engaging with this International Money Diary will not only increase your understanding of global financial practices but also inspire you with new ways to manage your money. You might discover a saving technique from Japan or a fun spending tradition from Brazil that you want to try.

Lastly, share your diary with friends or family. Discussing what you've learned can be a wonderful way to connect with others and spread the wisdom of financial literacy around the world. Your Money Diary could even be the start of an international conversation in your own home!

Remember, financial education is a journey, not a destination. By exploring the diverse ways children around the world save, spend, and think about money, you're taking valuable steps on your own path to becoming wise with your wealth. So, keep your diary close, your mind open, and continue to learn and grow. The world of money is vast and varied, and you're just beginning to uncover its secrets.

Your International Money Diary is more than just an activity; it's your passport to understanding and navigating the world's financial landscapes. So, treasure it, fill it with curiosity, and let it guide you towards making smart, informed money decisions. Who knows? Maybe one day, your money adventures will inspire a diary of their own. Happy exploring!

Chapter 11: Money and Happiness

Imagine embarking on a treasure hunt, where the treasure isn't gold or diamonds, but rather the joy and smiles money can bring when used wisely. In our journey through the land of finance, we've explored how to earn, save, and spend money. Now, let's dive into the heart of what truly matters: the relationship between money and happiness. Money, like a magical key, can open doors to new experiences, help us support the people we love, and even allow us to give to those in need. But here's a secret that even some adults haven't learned yet: happiness isn't measured by the size of your piggy bank or the number of toys in your room. Sometimes, the richest moments come from the simple joys—playing with a friend, sharing a homemade meal with your family, or giving a part of what you have to help someone else. These moments create sparks of happiness that can light up the world. In this chapter, we'll discover that while money can buy lots of things, the happiness it brings shines brightest when it's shared. We'll also see how finding your balance—between saving for your dreams, spending on what truly matters to you, and giving back—can turn your life into an adventure filled with happiness at every turn.

Can Money Buy Happiness?

Imagine you're on an adventure, hunting for the treasure of Happiness Island. You might think the key to unlocking this treasure is a chest full of gold or a wallet that never empties, but the map to true happiness is a bit more complicated. Sure, having enough money can make things easier - it means you can have a cozy place to live, yummy food, and even save up for a super cool bike. But think about it: have you ever gotten a toy you really wanted, only to find yourself bored with it a week later? That's because happiness isn't just about things; it's about experiences, friendships, and making memories. It's like planting a garden; money can buy the seeds (the things we want or need), but the joy comes from watching them grow, caring for them, and seeing the flowers bloom. It's the love, hard work, and time we put in that brings us the real happiness. So, while money is a helpful tool on our journey, it's not the only thing guiding our ship to Happiness Island.

Activity: Happiness Brainstorm
Now that we've explored the treasures and pitfalls of money, let's embark on a journey into the heart of happiness. What truly brings us joy? Is it something we can buy, or is it woven from the moments and memories we cherish? Gather your thoughts, for we're about to dive into the depths of happiness together.

Imagine a world where every smile, every laugh, and every moment of joy could be bottled up. What would your bottle contain? Let's start our Happiness Brainstorm by drawing an imaginary bottle or creating a list of things that fill you with happiness. But remember, these shouldn't be things you can buy with money. Think deeper. Perhaps it's the warmth of the sun on your face, or the thrill of climbing a tree to the very top. Maybe it's the quiet moments spent with a furry friend, or the magic of a story that transports you to another realm.

Happiness often blooms in the garden of kindness. Reflect on a time someone showed you kindness without expecting anything in return. How did it make you feel? Flip the coin - recall a moment you were kind to someone else. Paint these memories with words in your Happiness Bottle. These acts of kindness, no matter how small, can light up the dark corners of our hearts.

Adventures don't always require leaving the house. Sometimes, they happen in the kitchen with a recipe gone hilariously wrong, or in the backyard where a simple game turns into an epic quest. Add these adventure snippets to your bottle. They're reminders that happiness doesn't have an address; it's wherever we decide to find it.

Consider the friendships that brighten your life. Friends who've stood by you, shared secrets in whispered tones, and laughed until your bellies ached. These are the golden threads in the tapestry of happiness. Sketch these friendships into your brainstorm, honoring the bond that ties your hearts together.

In this brainstorm, also give space to the challenges you've faced. It might seem odd, finding happiness in challenges, but think about how you've grown because of them. Overcoming obstacles, learning new skills, or simply finding the courage to try again - these are victories that sculpt our spirits and stir a quiet happiness within us.

Let's not forget the simple, everyday wonders that often go unnoticed. The mystery of the stars at night, the story told by the clouds, the chorus of birds at dawn. These moments are free for all but owned by those who take the time to appreciate them. Dot your Happiness Bottle with these everyday marvels and watch how they start to sparkle.

As our brainstorm stretches and grows, you'll notice a pattern. True happiness isn't housed within a store; it can't be purchased, traded, or sold. It's woven from the intangible, the moments, and the memories we hold dear. It thrives in connections, adventure, kindness, overcoming, and the simple wonders of the world.

Now, look beyond your Happiness Bottle. Think about how you can create more of these moments. Can you seek out new adventures, forge deeper friendships, or find joy in the challenges that come your way? Happiness is an art, and you are the artist. With every choice, every action, you're painting your canvas with the colors of joy.

This activity isn't just an exercise; it's a map leading to true wealth, the kind that fills your heart and soul. As you journey forward in your understanding of money and its place in your life, remember this Happiness Brainstorm. Let it be a beacon, guiding you to choices that not only enrich your wallet but also your well-being.

In the chapters to come, we'll continue to explore the world of money, but let's carry the insights from this activity with us. Like a compass, it'll help us navigate through the storms and calms, always reminding us of what truly matters.

As you add the final touches to your Happiness Bottle, take a moment to appreciate its contents. This bottle, brimming with joy, adventure, and love, holds the essence of true happiness. And the best part? You can keep filling it, day after day, with new memories, new experiences, and new lessons learned.

Before we move on, here's a little challenge for you. Pick one item from your Happiness Bottle and make it your mission to experience it or create it for someone else in the coming week. It could be an act of kindness, a moment of adventure, or simply taking the time to appreciate an everyday wonder. Let's not just brainstorm happiness; let's live it and spread it.

As we wrap up this activity, remember that happiness is a labyrinth with many paths but no wrong turns. Every experience, every choice brings you closer to understanding what happiness means to you. Keep exploring, keep dreaming, and keep adding to your Happiness Bottle. The journey to happiness is infinite, and it's yours to discover.

Now, with our Happiness Bottles filled to the brim, let's step forward with hearts light and spirits high. The next chapter awaits, but we carry with us the treasures from our Happiness Brainstorm, ready to face the world with a newfound understanding of joy, money, and the delicate balance between the two.

Finding Your Balance

In the grande adventure of life, imagine you're on a boat sailing across an endless sea of possibilities. Money, like the sail, helps us move forward, but how we adjust our sail can make all the difference in the world. Think of finding your balance as the art of tuning your sail just right, so you're gliding smoothly through the waters. It's not just about stuffing your treasure chest; it's about making sure there's enough wind to take you to lands of joy and fulfillment. Imagine you're saving up for a video game or a new bike—yes, it feels epic once you get it, but remember, it’s the journey, the challenges you overcome, and the choices you make along the way that truly make you happier. By choosing wisely when to save, when to spend, and when to share your treasures, you create your own map to happiness. This magical balance is the secret treasure every young adventurer seeks in their quest for a happy life, with or without a chest full of gold.

Activity: The Feel-Good Budget Imagine having a treasure map that shows you where happiness hides. Wouldn't that be amazing? Now, let's pretend for a moment that money is a bit like that map, guiding us towards things that can make us smile. But, just like any adventure, we need to choose our path wisely. That's where the Feel-Good Budget comes into play. It's not just any budget; it's a special plan that helps us spend our money on things that truly make us happy.

First off, let's think about what makes us genuinely joyful. Is it spending time with friends? Buying a new book to read? Or maybe it's helping someone out? Whatever it is, jot them down. These are your happiness clues.

Now, let's get our explorer hats on. With our list of happiness clues, we're going to create a budget that's completely unique to you. This isn't about saving every penny or spending it all; it's about balance. A balance that makes your heart feel as full as your piggy bank.

First, we'll start with the basics. Picture your money as if it's a pie. (Who doesn't love pie, right?) This pie is made up of different slices, and each slice represents a part of your budget. We have slices for savings, giving, and, yes, spending on things that make you feel good.

For our Feel-Good Budget, we're going to focus on the spending slice today. This doesn't mean we forget about saving or giving. It just means we're shining the spotlight on spending wisely on what brings us joy.

Grab a piece of paper, and let's draw your pie. How big do you think each slice should be? Remember, there's no wrong answer here. It's all about what feels right for you.

Now, it's adventure time. With your list of happiness clues, start assigning a part of your spending slice to each one. Perhaps saving for a new skateboard brings you joy. Or maybe it's setting aside some money for a family movie night. See how your spending can create these joyful moments?

But here's the secret—a Feel-Good Budget isn't just about spending. It's also about seeing how giving and saving contribute to your happiness. Maybe saving for a goal gives you a sense of accomplishment. Or perhaps giving to a friend in need brings a smile to your face. Let's make sure your budget reflects these feelings too.

Remember, the goal isn't to spend all your money on fun things right away. It's about finding a happy balance. Sometimes, feeling good comes from waiting for something we really want and finally getting it. It makes the victory that much sweeter.

Another important part of our budgeting adventure is tracking our spending. Think of it as keeping a log on your treasure hunt. It helps us see if we're on the right path or if we need to adjust our map. There are fun tools and apps that can help with this, or you can simply use a notebook.

Sometimes we might slip up. Maybe we spend too much on something that didn't end up making us that happy. That's okay! Every explorer faces challenges. The important part is to learn from them and keep moving forward.

Now, it's time to set sail on your Feel-Good Budget journey. Remember, it's all about finding what makes you happiest and using your money to help you find more of that joy. It might take some experimenting, and that's part of the fun. Your budget is a living, breathing thing that grows with you.

Before we wrap up, let's dream a little. Imagine what your life could look like if you stick to your Feel-Good Budget. Picture the experiences, the adventures, and the smiles. Feels good, doesn't it?

In conclusion, creating a Feel-Good Budget is like crafting your own spell for happiness. It's putting your money to work in the most magical way—by using it to bring more joy, both to yourself and others. Keep tweaking your budget until it feels just right. And most importantly, have fun with it! After all, the journey to happiness is supposed to be an adventure, right?

What do you say, are you ready to chart your own course towards a happier life? Grab that treasure map, and let's get started. The path to joy is paved with the choices we make, and your Feel-Good Budget is the compass that will guide you there.

Chapter 12: Preparing for the Future

As we've ventured together through the twists and turns of financial literacy, from the basics of bucks to the joy of giving and the wisdom of wise spending, here we are at a pivotal chapter, "Preparing for the Future." Imagine standing at the edge of a grand, expansive forest. The trees are tall, the path is winding, and somewhere in that forest is your future. Now, you might think, "But how do I prepare for something I can't see?" Well, that's exactly what we're going to uncover. Preparing for the future isn't about predicting every step or avoiding every stumble; it's about packing your backpack with the right tools—dreams, goals, and skills—that you've been developing and will continue to hone. Whether you dream of becoming an astronaut, an artist, or an inventor, the journey requires you to set long-term goals, like creating your very own vision board that maps out your dreams, and building life-long money skills, such as writing a letter to your future self, reminding you of where you want to go and who you want to be. Remember, the future isn't a distant land that's light-years away; it's built on the steps you take today, each one a stone laid down on the path leading towards the horizon of your dreams.

Dream Big: Setting Long-term Goals

Imagine you're on a thrilling adventure, a quest for treasure that lies hidden, not on distant shores but within your own future. This treasure isn't gold or jewels; it's the dreams you hold closest to your heart, waiting to be discovered. In "Dream Big: Setting Long-term Goals," we'll step into the shoes of explorers, charting a course towards the aspirations that light up the night sky of our imaginations like constellations. Whether it's becoming an astronaut, a teacher, or even creating the next big video game, each goal is a star, guiding us forward. We'll learn that crafting our future starts with the seeds we plant today. Saving money might seem like a slow start, but it's like planting a magic bean that grows into a beanstalk reaching towering heights. It's about seeing beyond the immediate horizon and understanding that every penny saved is a step towards making those big dreams a reality. This journey is not just about reaching one goal; it's about setting sail towards a lifetime of adventures, armed with the knowledge that with patience, planning, and a dash of daring, we can navigate our way to any dream we dare to chase.

Activity: Vision Board Creation Imagine a place where all your dreams and goals live, a place you can see and touch, reminding you every day of where you're heading. In this chapter, we embark on a journey into the future, not with a time machine, but with something just as powerful: a vision board. A vision board is like a treasure map to your future, filled with pictures and words that represent your biggest dreams and goals.

First things first, let's gather our supplies. You'll need a poster board or a large piece of paper, magazines, scissors, glue, and markers or pens. If you have stickers or any other craft supplies you love, bring those along too. The more personal and fun you can make it, the better.

Before you start snipping pictures or drawing, take a moment to dream. Close your eyes and think about what you want your future to look like. What makes you happy? What are some things you want to do, places you wish to visit, or things you'd like to have? Remember, there are no limits in your imagination—dream big!

Now, open your eyes and start looking through magazines for pictures that match your dreams. If you dream of traveling to far-off places, find pictures of those destinations. If you wish to save enough money to buy a special toy, look for an image that represents that. It's not just about things you want to buy; think about activities that bring you joy, accomplishments you're proud of, or values that are important to you.

As you're cutting out pictures and words, think about how achieving these goals will make you feel. Happiness, pride, excitement—these feelings can also find a place on your vision board. You might even write down a few words that describe how you're going to feel when you accomplish your goals.

Next, arrange your pictures and words on your poster board. There's no right or wrong way to do this. You might choose to group similar goals together, create a big collage where everything blends together, or leave space between different dreams. What matters is that it makes sense to you and brings you joy when you look at it.

Once you're happy with your arrangement, it's time to glue everything in place. As you glue each piece, imagine yourself reaching that goal. It might sound silly, but visualization is a powerful tool. The more you can see and feel yourself achieving your dreams, the more motivated you'll be to make them come true.

With your vision board complete, hang it somewhere you'll see it every day. It could be near your bed, by your desk, or on the back of your door. Seeing your vision board regularly will keep your goals and dreams fresh in your mind. It's a daily reminder of what you're working towards and why.

Remember, your vision board isn't set in stone. As you grow and change, your dreams might too. Feel free to add new goals or adjust your board as you see fit. The important thing is that it remains a reflection of what you want and where you want to go.

Creating a vision board is more than just an art project; it's a step towards making your dreams a reality. Whether it's saving money, being kinder to others, learning a new skill, or anything else you dream of, your vision board is a map to your future. And every great adventure needs a map.

Now, I challenge you to share your vision board with someone you trust—maybe a parent, a sibling, or a friend. Explain to them what each picture or word represents. Sharing your dreams can be scary, but it also makes them feel more real. Plus, you'll have someone who can cheer you on and remind you of your dreams on days when they seem far away.

Remember, every day is a step closer to your dreams. Some days you might take giant leaps, and other days, tiny tiptoes. And that's okay. What's important is that you keep moving forward, keep dreaming, and keep believing in yourself. Your vision board isn't just a collection of pictures; it's a promise to yourself—a promise that your dreams are worth chasing.

So, as you look at your vision board today and every day after, remember that you have the power to turn those dreams into reality. It'll take patience, effort, and sometimes a bit of courage, but you've already taken the first step by creating your vision board. Keep dreaming, keep planning, and keep adventuring. The future is bright, and it's yours for the taking.

When the going gets tough, and it might, glance over at your vision board. Let it be a beacon of hope and a testament to your dreams. You're on an incredible journey, and with your vision board as your guide, there's no limit to what you can achieve. Happy dreaming, and here's to your future!

Money Skills for Life

Imagine you're on a thrilling adventure, where every decision you make impacts the journey ahead. Navigating this path requires a set of skills as powerful and magical as any treasure map for uncovering hidden gold. That's where money skills come into the dazzling light. Think of money as your trusty companion on this quest. Just like learning to master the ancient craft of map reading or deciphering mystical runes, understanding how to manage, save, and grow your money is a vital quest in itself. It's not just about counting coins or hoarding them away in a dragon-guarded vault. It's about making smart choices, like deciding when to save your gold for a more significant purchase or when to use it to help someone in need. And the secret is, as you become wiser with your money, you'll find it can lead you to realms you've only dreamed of. By setting out on this adventure now, you'll be equipped with the power to turn dreams into reality, ensuring your future is as bright and mighty as a hero's. So, take a deep breath, grab your adventurer's hat, and let's embark on the ultimate journey of mastering money skills for life. Just remember, the wisest adventurers know the importance of patience, practice, and persistence. Your treasure awaits!

Activity: Letter to My Future Self

Now, after exploring mountains of money wisdom and adventuring through valleys of financial facts, we've come upon a clearing bathed in the golden light of future possibilities. As we set up our camp here, it's time for a very special activity that's all about you and your journey ahead.

Imagine you're about to write a letter, not to a friend, but to someone who knows you better than anyone else does - your future self. Think of it as creating a treasure map, where 'X' marks your dreams and ambitions. But this map doesn't just point you to the treasure; it helps you create it.

First, let's think about what your paper and pen might say if they could talk. They'd say, "Fear not! We're here to carry your words from the realm of now into the vast oceans of tomorrow." So, grab those silent yet encouraging friends (your writing tools) and let's embark on this letter-writing quest.

Start with a greeting to your future self. Are you imagining yourself as a fearless explorer scaling the cliffs of success or a brilliant scientist uncovering miraculous money mysteries? Whatever you see, begin with a hello that fits your vision.

Next, dive into who you are in this present moment. Describe your current favorite activities, dreams, and maybe even your favorite ice cream flavor. It's these little snapshots that will remind your future self where you started from.

Now, sprinkle in your financial dreams and goals. Do you want to save enough money to buy that super-special something you've been dreaming of? Or maybe you're looking to save for college or to start your own business selling the world's juiciest lemonade. Write these goals down; they're the stars guiding your journey.

It's also important to share your worries and fears about money. Everyone has them, from kids to grown-ups. Writing them down can help you see that you're not alone and that you can overcome these hurdles one step at a time.

Of course, no treasure map is complete without advice to help navigate. Share some money tips you've learned, like the importance of saving or why needs must come before wants. These pearls of wisdom are the compass points leading you to your treasure.

Now, layer in some encouragement. Remind your future self that it's okay to make mistakes—they're just stepping stones on the path to success. Tell your future self to stay brave, curious, and always kind, especially when it comes to money decisions.

Here's where the magic of imagination comes to play. Dream up where you want to be in five, ten, or even fifteen years. Are you attending a top university, flying to the moon, or running your own charity? Whatever it is, paint this picture with your words. Let your hopes and dreams spill across the page, colorful and alive.

Add a dash of questions for your future self. Are you still in love with the same activities? Have your financial goals shifted? What's the most important lesson you've learned? These questions are seeds, and you'll be amazed at how they've grown when you finally read this letter in the future.

Before you sign off, make a promise to your future self. It could be to never give up on your dreams, to always make smart money choices, or to help others with their financial journeys. This promise is your anchor, keeping you grounded as you sail toward your dreams.

Finally, sign your letter with love and care. Seal it in an envelope and mark it with a "Do Not Open Until [future date]." Now, find a safe place to keep it, somewhere you know you'll remember.

In the years to come, this letter will be a time capsule, a message from the past that will remind you of your dreams, challenges, and growth. It's a way to see just how far you've traveled on your money adventure.

So, as we pack up our camp in this clearing and get ready to continue our journey, remember that this letter to your future self is more than just words on paper. It's a map, a promise, and a treasure all rolled into one, guiding you towards your brightest financial future.

As we say goodbye to this activity, know that every step you take, every decision you make, brings you one step closer to the dreams you've mapped out for yourself. Your future is as bright and as boundless as the stars above. So go forth, young adventurer, and create the future you envision with courage, wisdom, and a heart full of hope.

Conclusion

Well, here we are at the end of our amazing journey together. We've ventured through hills and valleys made of coins and paper bills, discovered the magic of saving, and the thrill of earning our own money. We learned how to tell the difference between what we need and what we wish for, how to make smart shopping decisions, and even how to grow our money through interest and simple investments. We've seen how giving can bring us joy and how important it is to balance saving, spending, and sharing. We've even peeked into how kids around the world manage their money and found out that, while money can't buy happiness, it can help us find a balance in life that does lead to happiness.

Remember, your money journey doesn't stop here. It's a big world out there, filled with opportunities to use what you've learned in new and exciting ways. Whether you're saving up for something special, planning to start your own mini-business, or dreaming about your future, the skills you've gained will help guide you. And just like any great adventure, there will be surprises and challenges along the way, but you're now better prepared to face them with confidence and wisdom. So take your next steps boldly, knowing that you have the tools to make your dreams a reality. The future is bright, and your journey is just beginning.

Recap: What We've Learned

Throughout this adventure, we've journeyed alongside Max the Money Mogul, uncovering the mysteries and magic of money management. We've learned that money isn't just paper and coins, but a tool that can help us achieve our dreams and secure our castles.

We started by understanding the basics of bucks—recognizing that whether it's cash, cards, or digital dollars, money is a means for exchanging value. From setting up a lemonade stand to making our first sale, we discovered how people earn money and the importance of having a budget.

The thrilling quest of saving taught us why storing our treasures for later is not only wise but necessary. We compared piggy banks to savings accounts, finding safe harbors for our hard-earned coins and learning about the magic of interest—how our money can grow while we sleep or while we're at school.

Our journey then took us to the realms of wise spending, where we learned to distinguish between needs and wishes. We navigated through markets with smart shopping tips, constantly reminded by Max that every wise decision leads us closer to our goals.

The Give, Save, Spend plan introduced a balance to our monetary world, teaching us the joy of spreading kindness through giving. We experienced firsthand that sharing with others brings a different kind of happiness, one that money can't buy.

As we ventured into earning our own money, our creativity was sparked. From mowing lawns to crafting jewelry, we explored various avenues to turn our talents into treasure. Setting financial goals became our map, guiding us towards our aspirations.

The lands of borrowing and lending showed us the importance of trust and responsibility. Engaging in the family bank loan simulation and the trust game, we learned valuable lessons about the respect and accountability that come with borrowing.

We then sailed through cyber seas, becoming money smart online. Max taught us to be vigilant, to recognize and avoid the pitfalls and scams that lurk in the shadows, aiming to snatch away our hard-earned loot.

Our expedition led us to the kingdom of budgeting, where we took control of our personal finances. Understanding prices and sales armed us with the knowledge to navigate through storms of spending, ensuring we always get the best value for our money.

Curiosity took us around the globe, as we learned about different currencies and how kids from distant lands save and spend. This not only broadened our horizons but also taught us the universal language of money.

The quest for happiness helped us understand that while money is important, it's not the key to happiness. Finding balance and appreciating the simple joys life offers creates a treasure chest brimming with happiness.

As we prepare for future adventures, dreaming big and setting long-term goals are our North Stars. We learned to envision our future, understanding that with patience, dedication, and smart money management, we can achieve anything.

And so, we stand at the threshold, looking back on the knowledge we've gained and the challenges we've overcome. Max's teachings have equipped us with the tools we need to navigate the seas of life, making wise and informed decisions about our finances.

But remember, the journey doesn't end here. The seas of financial knowledge are vast and ever-changing. There are always new skills to learn, new goals to chase, and new adventures to embark on. As we take our next steps in this journey, let's carry forward the lessons learned and the spirit of adventure that guided us thus far.

May your paths be paved with gold, may your chests never empty, and may you always find joy in the journey. Here's to endless quests, to lifelong learning, and to a future brighter than the most sparkling treasure. Onward, to your money journey!

Taking Your Next Steps in Your Money Journey

As we close this adventure of coins and currency, it's time to lace up your shoes for the journey ahead. Picture your path shimmering with possibilities, each step a chance to make your money grow and glow. It's not just about spending wisely but making each penny count toward building the future of your dreams.

Think of all the stories where heroes embark on quests, discovering treasures and learning lessons along the way. That's you on your money journey. Except, instead of dragons, you might face temptations to spend on things you don't need, or hurdles like saving enough for something special. But, like any valiant hero, you've got what it takes to overcome these challenges.

Your journey will be filled with decisions. Some will be easy, like choosing between saving for a new game or a bike. Others might be trickier, requiring you to think about what you truly value. Remember, each choice crafts your journey, making it uniquely yours.

Just as a map guides explorers, your budget is your treasure map. It shows you where your money comes from, where it's going, and how you can navigate toward your financial goals. Whether it's a budget for a week, a month, or a year, use it to plot your course.

Now, think about your savings as a magical garden. The seeds you plant today are the savings you set aside. With patience and care, these savings will grow, blossoming into a future where you can afford the things that matter most. Always look for opportunities to add to your garden, whether it's from birthday money, chores, or a lemonade stand.

Imagine stepping into the shoes of a wise investor. Your journey might lead you to learn about stocks, bonds, or even starting a small business. These are paths that can help your money multiply over time. Just remember, the aim isn't to become rich overnight but to ensure a secure and bright future.

Along the way, you'll find joy in sharing. Allocating a part of your treasure to help others not only brings happiness but teaches us the value of community and support. Look for causes you believe in and consider how you can contribute.

Remember, your journey is about balance. It's okay to spend on things that bring you joy, as long as you're meeting your saving and sharing goals. Think of it as planning an epic feast. You'd want a bit of everything on your plate, right? Your finances are much the same.

Be curious and seek knowledge. Just as adventurers learn from the lands they explore, continue to learn about money. Read books, ask questions, and maybe even start a money club with friends. There's always more to discover, and knowledge is the best tool in your arsenal.

Even the bravest explorers sometimes need a guide. Don't hesitate to ask for advice from parents, teachers, or mentors. They can offer maps and compasses in the form of wisdom and experience, helping you avoid pitfalls and traps on your path.

Set milestones along your journey. These will be your personal landmarks, like saving for that special toy or donating to a cause you care about. Celebrating these achievements will keep you motivated and excited about what lies ahead.

Most importantly, believe in yourself. Like the heroes of old, you have the power to shape your destiny. Your beliefs, decisions, and actions will guide you through the mazes of finance, leading to a future bright with promise.

As you stand at this beginning, eager to step forward, remember that every great journey starts with a single step. Each penny saved, each wise choice, each moment of generosity, leads you closer to your dreams.

Your money journey is more than just numbers and notes; it's a quest for wisdom, freedom, and happiness. As you advance, keep your head high, your heart open, and your mind ready for the adventures that await.

Now, go forth, young adventurer. Your journey awaits, filled with mysteries to uncover, dragons to tame (in the form of financial challenges), and treasures to discover. The path might twist and turn, but remember, with courage, wisdom, and a dash of fun, there's no limit to what you can achieve on your money journey.

Appendix A: Appendix

Welcome to the appendix, the treasure chest at the end of our financial adventure! Think of this section as your secret map, filled with clues and tools to help you navigate through the world of money with ease and confidence.

An Adventure Recap

Let's take a moment to remember the incredible journey we've been on. We explored the basics of bucks, discovered the importance of saving, and learned how to make our money grow. We became wise spenders, learned to give generously, and even found out how to earn our own money. Then, we tackled borrowing and lending, protecting our money, and even took a whirlwind tour of money around the world. And who could forget diving into the relationship between money and happiness?

The Toolbox

Within these pages, you'll find a toolkit, not of hammers and nails, but of ideas, tips, and tricks to build your financial future. From setting up your first savings account to planning your very own giving project, each tool you've gathered along the way is meant to build on each other, creating a foundation as strong as a fortress.

- **Activities Recap:** Listed here are all the activities we journeyed through. Use them as stepping stones to revisit and strengthen concepts you've learned.

- **Money Terms Glossary:** A treasure chest of terms that we encountered on our journey. It's always handy to have a glossary at your fingertips when navigating the seas of financial lingo.

- **Resources for Further Learning:** Are you ready to expand your horizons? Here, you'll find books, websites, and games approved by Max the Money Mogul himself, to take your financial education to even greater heights.

- **Answers to Activities:** Curious to know how you did on the activities? Turn here to check your answers and understand where you shine the brightest.

Your Next Adventure

Remember, every great adventurer needs a trusty map, and this appendix is yours. Use it to guide your way as you continue to explore the vast, exciting world of money. Just as every explorer keeps their tools polished and ready, use this appendix to keep your financial knowledge sharp.

And finally, always remember that the greatest treasure is the journey itself. Each step you take in understanding money not only brings you closer to your financial goals but also to becoming the courageous, wise, and kind-hearted adventurer you are meant to be. So, keep exploring, keep dreaming, and above all, keep building your path to a bright and prosperous future.

Happy adventures, young explorer!

Glossary of Money Terms

Embark on a quest through the jungle of money terms, where every word is a stepping stone to becoming a wise money champion. As you've journeyed through the chapters, you've encountered numerous landmarks and mystical creatures, from "Savings" to "Investments." Now, in the heart of this adventure, let's uncover the treasure map that deciphers these magical terms.

ATM (Automated Teller Machine)

An ATM is like a vending machine, but instead of snacks, it gives you money. It's a wizard box where you use your magic card to withdraw your gold coins.

Bank

Think of a bank as a giant piggy bank, where instead of one person, an entire town can keep their money safe. It's like a castle that guards your treasure against dragons.

Budget

A budget is your personal treasure map. It shows you how much gold you have and plans out your adventures, so you don't spend it all in one place.

Credit Card

This magical card lets you borrow gold from the bank to buy what you need now and pay back later. But be careful, if you don't return the gold on time, the bank asks for extra!

Debt

Debt is when you owe someone money. It's like having a monkey on your back until you can return the bananas you borrowed.

Interest

Interest works two ways. When you save money in the bank, they pay you extra as a thank you. But if you borrow, you pay them extra. It's like planting a money tree; the more you care for it, the more fruits you get.

Invest

Investing is like sending your money on quests to find more treasure. Sometimes it brings back lots of gold, and sometimes it doesn't. It's a way to make your money grow over time.

Savings Account

A savings account at a bank is your safe treasure chest. It keeps your money safe, and it might even grow a little if you leave it there long enough.

Taxes

Taxes are like a portion of your treasure that you share with the kingdom to help build roads, schools, and keep the kingdom running. Everyone pitches in a bit of their gold for the greater good.

This glossary is your enchanted book to understand the magic of money. With each term you learn and use, you're on your way to becoming not just a money wizard, but a money hero. Remember, it's not just about saving your treasure, but also about making it grow, spending wisely, and sharing some of it for good causes. May your journey be filled with prosperity and wise choices!

Resources for Further Learning

By now, you've journeyed through the wondrous lands of saving, spending, and growing your money. It's been quite an adventure, hasn't it? But remember, every great explorer needs a map and a compass. In your quest to become a Money Mogul like Max, seeking out resources to fuel your journey is both wise and essential. Let me introduce you to some magical tools and tales to guide you on your path forward.

Imagine a library, its shelves bursting with books, each cover more inviting than the last. This is where your adventure continues. There are tales of young heroes and heroines, just like you, facing dragons of debt and mountains of money mysteries. Seek out stories that reveal the secrets of saving and the puzzles of pocket money. Every book is a doorway to a new adventure in learning.

But wait, there's a room beyond the library, illuminated by the glow of screens. Here, in the vast expanse of the digital world, websites await your curiosity. With a click, you can uncover interactive games that turn the chore of learning into a challenge as thrilling as any quest. These games let you build virtual lemonade stands or navigate through shopping challenges, each click bringing you closer to mastering your money.

Ah, but an explorer is never alone. Gather your fellow adventurers—friends, family, and educators—and start a club. Together, you can embark on treasure hunts for knowledge, share your discoveries, and even invite wise guides (like financial educators) to share their maps and tools. There's strength in numbers, and learning alongside others makes the journey all the more rewarding.

Now, picture a notebook, its pages empty but for a question that sparks a fire in your mind. Use it to jot down your thoughts, your dreams, and yes, your questions about money. This notebook becomes a personal treasure chest, filled with your own insights and revelations. And sometimes, the act of writing can lead to finding answers within yourself.

Remember, your journey is continuous, like the winding path of a river. There are podcasts that sing the songs of financial literacy in your ears, guiding you gently along the way. Listening to stories of others' adventures with money can inspire you, offer lessons, and light up paths you might not have seen before.

In your quest, you'll meet wise mentors and fellow travelers, each with their own tales of triumph and trials. Seek out mentors who have sailed these waters before you. Their experiences, shared over cups of hot chocolate or through letters, can be lighthouses guiding you away from financial folly towards the shores of success.

Your magic doesn't end in these pages. Technology offers you apps designed to make saving as thrilling as discovering buried treasure. With each amount you save, imagine you're building your own castle, stone by stone, until one day you stand atop its towers, surveying the kingdom of your financial security.

Embark on quests that challenge you to apply what you've learned. Whether it's a simulated stock market game or a budgeting challenge with your friends, each victory, each stumble, is a step towards mastery.

And for those moments when the path seems shrouded in mist, remember that workshops and seminars are like the gatherings of old, where travelers would exchange maps and compasses. Attending a workshop can equip you with new tools and new courage to face the challenges ahead.

As you move forth, create a montage of your journey. Use videos, blogs, or a simple scrapbook to document your adventures in money management. Looking back on your progress can be a powerful reminder of how far you've come, and a motivator for how far you still wish to go.

Peer beneath the surface of every experience and lesson. Reflection is a powerful tool for growth. After each endeavor, take a moment to ponder what went well and what could have been done differently. This reflection turns experience into wisdom.

And finally, remember, every hero has a story, and yours is just beginning. Your financial education is a canvas, and you hold the brush. Paint it with broad strokes and daring colors. Make it a masterpiece of learning, adventure, and triumph.

So, keep your wits about you, your resources at hand, and embark on your continuing adventure with a heart full of courage and a mind open to learning. The world of financial literacy is vast and filled with wonders waiting to be discovered. Your journey has just begun, and the paths to explore are endless. Go forth, young explorer, and conquer the world of money with knowledge, wisdom, and joy.

Answers to Activities

Remember the lemonade stand we talked about? If you decided to save some of your earnings each time, you might have noticed your "business" money growing, even without selling more lemonade! It's just like planting a seed and watching it sprout into a flower. That was your first taste of why saving is super important.

Next, we dove into the idea of a special toy fund. Did you find out how long it would take to save for your toy? This activity was aimed at teaching you patience and the thrill of hitting a saving goal. You were a savings superhero, even if it felt slow at times. It's about gathering little by little to reach something big.

When exploring places to keep your money, you learned that while piggy banks are great, savings accounts in banks are like secure treasure chests that add interest. It's like your money making more money just by being there, like magic!

In the land of investments with our stock market game, it was all pretend, but the lessons were real. You learned that investing could be a way to make your money work hard, just like you would in a lemonade stand, but always with a risk.

Budgeting for a birthday party might have shown you that sometimes, we have to choose—maybe a magician over an extra-large cake. Wise spending means making choices that let us have fun while staying within our treasure map bounds.

Creating your Give, Save, Spend jars was a big step into managing money like a pro. You saw firsthand how dividing your money can help you manage it better, ensuring you always have enough for what you truly value.

The joy of giving chapter highlighted that sharing your treasure can bring happiness not just to others but to you too. Planning a giving project probably opened your eyes to the warmth of helping and the joy it spreads, like sunshine.

Starting your mini business, even on paper, was like being the captain of your own ship. Did you find exciting ways to earn coins? This activity was all about seeing opportunities for earning around you.

Setting goals with Max was about aiming for the stars. Whether your goal was a new game or saving for college, it was about lighting that fire of ambition inside you and charting a course towards your dreams.

In our pretend family bank, borrowing money came with responsibility. The trust game later showed how paying back on time helps in keeping relationships strong, like an invisible bond of trust.

Navigating online safely through our Cyber Smart Quiz was like being a detective, spotting potential traps and learning to protect your digital treasure chest from pirates lurking in the vast ocean of the internet.

Spot the Scam with Max might have been eye-opening! Fraudsters are the modern-day bandits, and you learned how to outsmart them, keeping your money safe by being aware and cautious.

Max's Monthly Budget Challenge was a dive into the world of numbers, finding balance like a tightrope walker between what comes in and what goes out. This showed you how budgets can be a map to guide your spending.

The Currency Conversion Contest whisked you away on a global adventure, teaching you the diversity of money around the world. It's like discovering new lands, understanding that while the look of money can change, its value is what matters.

Finally, envisioning your future with a vision board was your step into the realm of dreams. Here, you learned that money is but a tool to help shape your future, bringing dreams within reach, one wise decision at a time.

Through these activities, you've journeyed far and wide across the lands of money wisdom. Take these lessons with you as you continue to grow, exploring the vast world of finance with curiosity, courage, and care. Remember, every small step today is a leap towards your grandest dreams tomorrow.

Printed in Great Britain
by Amazon

39119670R00081